Praise for *Ultimate Memory Magic*

"In his powerful new book, *Ultimate Memory Magic,* Jim teaches you his proven secrets to boost memory, mood, and relationships. I know millions of people will be able to benefit from his wisdom."
—Dr. Daniel G. Amen

"Jim Karol is the most amazing mentalist on the planet! His extraordinary memory and mental abilities are beyond belief."
—George Noory, *Coast to Coast AM*

"Jim Karol is a gifted mentalist who is dedicated to helping people improve their cognitive abilities and emotional intelligence."
—Neil E. Grunberg, Ph.D., Professor of Neuroscience and Clinical Psychology at Uniformed Services University

"As the founder of the USA Memory Championship, I can affirm that Jim Karol is the 'Holy Grail' that neuroscientists are looking for in their research about the unlimited power of the human brain! Jim's new book, *Ultimate Memory Magic,* is an essential read for *anyone* desiring to improve their memory and cognitive health."
—Tony Dottino, president of Dottino Consulting Group

"Simply put, I've never met anyone like Jim Karol. I've had the privilege of traveling the world entertaining our troops with Jim and seen firsthand his memory and mental abilities, which are truly from another planet. I tip my cap to anyone who takes the time to go on a USO tour, but then there are people who are a cut above, who really leave an impression because they put so much passion into what they do. Jim has that passion, both for his craft and for our troops. It's a really beautiful thing because passion like his can't be faked. *Ultimate Memory Magic* is a must-read for anyone who wants to improve their mind, and their life!"

—Robert Irvine, chef, fitness authority,
philanthropist, and author of *Fit Fuel*

ULTIMATE MEMORY MAGIC

ULTIMATE MEMORY MAGIC

The Transformative Program
for Sharper Memory, Mental Clarity,
and Greater Focus . . . at Any Age!

✦

JIM KAROL
with Michael Ross

Foreword by **Daniel G. Amen, M.D.,**
Bestselling Author of *Memory Rescue*

ST. MARTIN'S
ESSENTIALS
New York

The information in this book is not intended to replace the advice of the reader's own physician or other medical professional. You should consult a medical professional in matters relating to health, especially if you have existing medical conditions, and before starting, stopping or changing the dose of any medication you are taking. Individual readers are solely responsible for their own health care decisions. The author and the publisher do not accept responsibility for any adverse effects individuals may claim to experience, whether directly or indirectly, from the information contained in this book.

www.stmartins.com

Library of Congress Cataloging-in-Publication Data

Names: Karol, Jim, author. | Ross, Michael, author.
Title: Ultimate memory magic : the transformative program for sharper memory, mental clarity, and greater
   focus . . . at any age! / Jim Karol with Michael Ross ; foreword by Daniel G. Amen, M.D.
Description: First. | New York : St. Martin's Essentials, 2019. | Includes bibliographical references.
Identifiers: LCCN 2019026297 | ISBN 9781250221919 (trade paperback) |
   ISBN 9781250221926 (ebook)
Subjects: LCSH: Memory. | Self-care, Health. | Brain—Popular works.
Classification: LCC BF371 .K167 2019 | DDC 153.1/2—dc23
LC record available at https://lccn.loc.gov/2019026297

Our books may be purchased in bulk for promotional, educational, or business use. Please contact your local bookseller or the Macmillan Corporate and Premium Sales Department at 1-800-221-7945, extension 5442, or by email at MacmillanSpecialMarkets@macmillan.com.

First Edition: September 2019

10 9 8 7 6 5 4 3 2 1

For all the wounded warriors, veterans,
and active-duty military around the world.
Thank you for your service.

✦

Contents

✦

Foreword

✦

Your brain is like a muscle. The more you use it, the more you can continue using it. New learning leads to new connections in the brain, which will enhance your memory. No learning causes the brain to start breaking its internal connections. No matter what your age, mental exercise has a global, positive effect on the brain.

In four decades of brain research, neuroscientist Marian Diamond, Ph.D., from the University of California, Berkeley, has helped revolutionize the way we think about brain health. In a lecture to the American Society on Aging, she said, "We now know that with proper stimulation and an enriched environment, the human brain can continue to develop at any age."

Mentalist Jim Karol is the human embodiment of Dr. Diamond's research. Jim grew up in Allentown, Pennsylvania, where he was a mediocre student in high school and even bullied because of his large frame. He attended a local college and ended up working in a steel mill. At the age of twenty-nine he hurt his knees and was laid off at the mill. It was then that he started working in a magic shop, where he discovered he had a talent for it. At thirty-one, he started performing magic shows and word spread about this "madman of magic." Before he knew it, Jim found himself on the front pages of newspapers across the country for correctly predicting the

Pennsylvania lottery. He was asked to appear on several television shows and his popularity began to grow. He became a hit on college campuses and was even invited to the White House.

At fifty, Jim had a health crisis and was diagnosed with cardio-myopathy and an enlarged heart. His doctor told Jim his heart looked like that of his ninety-three-year-old mother, and there was nothing to do but "enjoy the ride." Unsatisfied with the prognosis, Jim started a course of physical therapy. While he was riding a stationary bike, instead of watching TV, he started to use his mind. This average man started to memorize the states and their capi-tals, more than 80,000 zip codes, every word in the Scrabble dic-tionary, and the thousands of digits of Pi. Jim can tell you the day of the week for *every* date, all the way back to 1 A.D., and can mem-orize a shuffled deck of cards in less than a minute!

I met Jim through a mutual friend at Andrews Air Force Base when he was headed overseas on a USO tour to entertain the troops. Watching him memorize a shuffled deck of cards and then guess which card I had picked in my mind, completely blew me away. As I got to know Jim, it became clear that he was focused on growing his brain. "Memory athlete" is a term that was coined for people like Jim, who are adept at these kinds of memory feats. Now, exciting new research from Stanford University School of Medicine and the Max Planck Institute in Munich has shown that mnemonic train-ing, one of the methods favored by memory athletes, can be success-fully taught to people without any special memory skills, and that it "bulks up the brain's memory networks." The study participants, who used the technique to memorize lists of seventy-two words, were able to recall seventy-one, on average, twenty minutes afterward and had similar results when they were retested four months later.

The best mental exercises involve acquiring new knowledge and doing things you haven't done before. Even if your routine activities are fairly complicated, such as teaching a college course, reading brain scans, or fixing a crashed computer network, they won't help your brain as much as learning something new. Whenever the brain does something over and over, it learns how to do it using less and less energy. New learning, such as learning zip codes, the Scrabble dictionary, a new hobby or game, helps to establish new connections, thus maintaining and improving the function of other less-often-used brain areas.

Jim's new book *Ultimate Memory Magic* is a treasure of powerful information that can help supercharge your brain, transform your life, and even improve your relationships.

—Daniel G. Amen, M.D.
Founder, Amen Clinics
Author of *Memory Rescue* and *Change Your Brain, Change Your Life*

Introduction

Becoming Smarter, Sharper, and Much More Alert

✦

Fifty-seven-year-old Brian was a real estate broker who struggled to remember a client's name, and especially a face. "Forgetting someone's name, or worse, not recognizing them altogether, are cardinal sins in my business," he said.

This Chicago native knew that success in sales hinged on success with people. How could he make connections if he simply couldn't remember details? Lately, Brian's faulty memory had progressed from an occasional nuisance—like losing his keys and misplacing his phone—to a daily chore of struggling to connect with clients and make a sale. "I worry that I'm losing my edge," he said. "I worry that my mind isn't as sharp as it used to be. Am I suffering from the early stages of Alzheimer's disease? Can I recover from these setbacks? I'm still too young for old age to be setting in—so what's going on?"

Carla of Norfolk, Virginia, had asked herself similar questions.

"I'm a lieutenant in the United States Navy who has been entrusted with countless details," the thirty-eight-year-old said. "Yet I feel like I have brain fog. I'm exhausted all the time, and I can't hold a thought in my head. Even worse, I'm filled with so much negativity. Anxious thoughts range from mere twinges of uneasiness to full-blown panic attacks. Sometimes I experience rapid heartbeat, trembling, sweating, and queasiness. I'm still young, but I'm just not sharp. Is there such thing as a mind makeover—and can I have one?"

Don was a forty-four-year-old high school teacher in Los Angeles. Recent battles with weight gain, low energy, not to mention a health scare, had convinced him that his life could, and should, be better. "Up to this point, my students have always kept me feeling young," the science teacher explained. "All that changed when I was rushed to the ER with symptoms of a heart attack."

As it turned out, Don was experiencing the effects of stress and middle age, not heart disease. But in spite of feeling relieved, he knew his life couldn't return to business as usual. "I'm only a middle-aged man, which means I have a whole lot of living ahead of me," he said. "Yet I feel as if I have one foot in the grave. Stress is so overwhelming, I think I'm losing my mind. I'm not the sharp science guy that my students once enjoyed being around. I need to change my life, but I don't know where to start."

Kathy recently retired from her thirty-five-year career with the United States Postal Service. The Atlanta, Georgia, native had just turned sixty-eight and decided it was time to slow down. But after just six months into her long-awaited life of leisure, Kathy began experiencing a brand-new (and highly unwanted) dilemma: boredom.

"I hate retirement," she confided. "While my job kept me on my toes, at least all that social interaction kept me alert. Suddenly, I'm bored and irritable, and I constantly lose things—including my thoughts! Instead of enjoying the so-called golden years, I seem to be fading into the sunset. I want my life back!"

Ready for a Mind Makeover?

Four people, four stories—yet one common struggle: diminishing brain power.

Just like millions of other Americans, Brian, Carla, Don, and Kathy don't feel as sharp as they once were. They misplace items, forget simple details, fumble with people's names, and find themselves in a depressing fog—constantly feeling tired, anxious, sad, and one step behind the rest of the world.

Can you relate? Do you feel as if you're merely existing day after day . . . instead of thriving? Day after day, you're probably reminded that so much is on the line: relationships, health, careers, relevance, self-confidence . . . quality of life.

If all this rings true, you're not alone. Without even realizing it, here's what's going on inside each of our bodies:

◆ *Aging Immune Systems.* As we grow older, our immune systems usually start turning against us, attacking the body's own tissues instead of the various viruses and bacteria they are supposed to fight. In other words, our joints become arthritic, our bones brittle, our arteries clogged, our brains foggy, our lung capacities shrunk, and our muscle strength diminished. According to medical experts, nearly every disease of aging is associated with immune hyperactivity, and this hyperactivity is largely responsible for human aging itself.

◆ *Increased Stress.* Anxious thoughts swirl through our brains when we're tired, when we're sick, when we're inching our way through morning traffic, and when we're late for an important meeting. Fear kicks in as our safety is threatened and our circumstances slide out of control. Suddenly, our brains go on full alert, launching into a fight-or-flight state . . . surging adrenaline through our veins. (No need for that double-shot supersize caffeine concoction!) But here's what's most unsettling: The fear-worry-stress cycle is on the rise in America. It is often at the heart of overeating, alcoholism, cigarette smoking, drug abuse, and a long list of other compulsive behaviors. Here's yet another unsettling thought: Over the span of our lifetimes, stress and worry account for hours and hours of invaluable time that we'll never get back. Stress blocks our creativity, hinders concentration, and robs our joy and contentment. Therefore, it is critical we come down from the hills of stress and into the valleys of rest on a daily basis. Our bodies are not designed for a continual state of fear, worry, and anxiety—but instead for continual tranquility with short bursts of adrenaline.[1]

+ *Decreased Memory.* According to the National Institute of Mental Health, as we age, many of us experience problems with memory and concentration—officially called Age Associated Memory Impairment. However, memory problems can affect people of all ages, all backgrounds, all walks of life . . . and from every corner of the globe. So here's the bottom line for everyone: That fog we often feel trapped in is very real. Changes in brain function can interfere with our ability to perform our jobs, pursue our interests, or even engage in social activities.

From aging immune systems and increased stress to decreased memories, a war is being waged inside our bodies. A myriad of weapons are attacking us on so many fronts. But before we lose hope and throw in the towel, we need a dose of reality: There *is* hope.

We can actually reverse the damage.[2]

My own story proves that it's never too late, and we're never too old to improve our health. Serious heart conditions, debilitating diseases, sky-high blood pressure, out-of-control cholesterol, obesity—regardless of the issue, we can take that first step and do something positive to reclaim our bodies. It's the same with our minds.

We *can* preserve and even enhance our memory and other aspects of mental function. Concentration, alertness, and the ability to focus can be strengthened, leading to improvements in problem-solving ability, productivity, and even IQ.

Here's the first thing we need to understand: Our mind, body, and emotions are interconnected. Obviously, I inhabit a physical body. And the health of my body is connected to my Emotional Self, as well as my "soulful" self. So in order to get back a sharp mind and get on the path to good health, I need to treat my *entire* body. Those obsessive thoughts—the judgmental ones and the negative self-talk that goes on inside my head—can affect how I feel. This, in turn, can affect my body.

Consider the stomach, for example. It can act as a second brain when it comes to worrying. According to Dr. Oz (Mehmet Oz, M.D.), just like our brains, "our stomachs have their own nervous systems, called the enteric nervous system. When we worry, millions of receptors embedded in the gastrointestinal tract react to fear by speeding up or slowing down our digestion, which can lead to nausea, diarrhea, and heartburn."[3]

Theologian and writer Elouise Renich Fraser, Ph.D., says this about our physical bodies—*and* the effects of stress: "My body, once ignored and despised, has become an ally in the reorientation of my internal and external life. It lets me know when I'm running away, avoiding yet another of God's invitations to look into my past and the way it binds me as a theologian. I can't trust my mind as often as I trust my body. My mind tries to talk me into business as usual, but my body isn't fooled. Insomnia, intestinal pain, and diarrhea let me know there's work to be done."[4]

This mind-body-emotions connection is where we'll begin our discussion.

Cluing in to this reality and understanding the war being waged in my body unlocked the answers I needed. My destiny wasn't a wheelchair, nor was it a future staring at the beige walls of a hospital room. I was determined to get on with living, which meant . . .

- ✦ Sharpening my thinking and regaining my mental edge
- ✦ Living free from disease
- ✦ Getting in the best physical shape of my life
- ✦ Clearing away negativity and stress
- ✦ Becoming more creative

Brain Boot Camp Starts Now!

Welcome to my Cogmental Intelligence Program!

Within these pages, I combine the best of Emotional Intelligence with the study of mentalism, memory, cognition, and the art of deception detection—revealing that a stronger mind, a better body, and a transformed life is never out of reach for anyone. I'll take you on a journey from my days as a steelworker to becoming what experts say is "one of the most extraordinary minds in the world."

My Cogmental Intelligence training has been used to help professional athletes, business leaders, law enforcement, and military veterans. From enhancing memory and focus to boosting intuition and self-esteem, my program has gained the support of memory experts. Take a look at this: "I wanted to reiterate how profoundly your presentation impacted the neuroscience community here at MIT, particularly the faculty members who study memory! Indeed, in historical terms, you may possess one of the greatest long-term memories ever documented." (Robert Ajemian, Ph.D., Research Scientist, McGovern Institute for Brain Research, MIT)

SOME QUICK DEFINITIONS AS WE BEGIN

Emotional Intelligence (EI): In a nutshell, this popular technique is a way of connecting with and relating to people on a deeper level. It's all about having the ability to identify our own and other people's emotions, understand them, and be able to manage them. There are solid benefits to increasing our EI, including improved mental health, better job performance, and better relationships. Four key principles drive Emotional Intelligence:

1. *Self-Awareness*—recognizing our own emotions
2. *Self-Control*—calmly managing our emotions
3. *Empathy*—considering another person's feelings and perspective
4. *Social Awareness*—improving communication skills

Cogmental Intelligence (CI): I coined this phrase and developed a program that combines the best of EI with the study of mentalism, memory, cognition, and deception detection. My program studies the inner workings of the brain in order to make it more powerful. Four key principles drive Cogmental Intelligence:

1. *Mentalism*—exploring perception and reality and how they can be affected by mind tricks
2. *Memory*—reproducing or recalling what has been learned and retained in our minds

3. *Cognition*—acquiring knowledge and understanding through thought, experience, and the senses

4. *Reading Others*—cluing in to nonverbal communication such as facial expressions, body posture, gestures, eye movement, and the use of space

Deception Detection: This is a fascinating study of body language that seeks to uncover reliable behavioral indicators of deception—and it's a big part of my program. It's a tough skill to acquire, and not everyone can master it. Yet those who do end up possessing a powerful key to unlocking the motives of others. Basically, it involves the examination of behaviors such as posture shifts, gaze aversion, and foot and hand movements. One of the skills of deception detection is the ability to recognize the unspoken subtext of a conversation, as well as the ability to *hear* emotion. This is an invaluable study for anyone in law enforcement, teaching professions, and sales.

Memitation: This is my own unique mental exercise that mixes meditation with memorization. I define it this way: *The act of reviewing memorized information in quiet thought, while focusing on breathing.*

HOW TO GET THE MOST FROM THIS BOOK

The aim of *Ultimate Memory Magic* is to help you discover and apply your own potential for a more powerful mind and, at the same time, to help you improve your health, your relationships, your career, and your overall quality of life. It begins when we change our thinking from "I can't" to "I can"—to thinking creatively and boundlessly—and determine to start achieving what we never, ever thought we could accomplish in life.

Through practical physical and mental exercises, I'll guide you with breakthrough thinking principles that can help you sharpen your edge for real-world results. My Cogmental Intelligence and deception detection techniques will enable you to unlock the motives of others for stronger interpersonal connections and greater influence—at home and at work.

Here's what you'll find in these pages, along with my tips on how to get the most out of each topic we'll explore.

Part One: A Better Mind at *Any* Age

✓ Your Brain Can Improve (I'm Living Proof)

We'll begin our conversation with three secrets that changed my life: (1) my brain can improve, (2) my health can improve, and (3) my quality of life can improve.

Tip: *As you read this chapter, think about what keeps you from reaching your goals.* Consider how you can remove those barriers. For example, are you held back by fear, insecurity, wounds from the past, or negativity?

✓ Myth-Buster: "I'm Not Smart Enough"

I share my own journey from unmotivated steelworker to memory expert. I tell how I struggled with bullies all through high school, even as an adult. Improving my brain was the first step toward improving my life. And guess what? Change is possible for every man and woman—regardless of our age and our circumstances.

Tip: *Think about your own dreams.* Who did you want to be when you grew up? If you haven't yet reached that dream, how can you still become that person today?

✓ **Myth-Buster: "I'm Too Weak"**

Twenty years ago, I was a depressed steelworker in Allentown, Pennsylvania—broke, stuck, stressed, and in the worst shape of my life. Today, I've learned that as I clear away stress and negativity, and as I get my muscles moving and my heart pumping through exercise, I feel better. And after a vigorous workout, my mind is recharged too.

Tip: *Think about your own health.* What steps can you take to improve? What can give you the courage to get started . . . and motivate you to keep going? Is negativity blocking you? Are you battling stress and anxiety?

✓ **Myth-Buster: "I'm Too Old"**

You'll learn from my story that I'm now stronger, smarter, and more alive—in my sixties! It's never too late to improve our bodies and our minds. Nothing is stopping any of us from having a better quality of life. The sad fact is, we are our own worst enemies. We limit ourselves and block all the possibilities before us. Two things have given me the motivational fuel I need to improve: I've learned to think both creatively and boundlessly.

Tip: *Think about where you are in your life.* How can you become a better version of yourself? What is one simple step you can take in a positive direction?

Part Two: My Memory Magic Plan

✓ **Welcome to the World of Cogmental Intelligence**

As we head down a path to a more powerful mind, we'll nurture the mind-body-emotions connection, as well. My program focuses on treating our *entire* body.

`Tip:` *Think about your people skills.* Are you good at reading people? (Why or why not?) Think of at least one step you can take to improve each of these areas: (1) self-awareness, (2) self-management, (3) social awareness, and (4) relationship management.

✓ Brain-Booster No. 1: Enhance Memory and Sharpen Focus

We'll explore brain games that exercise our gray matter. At least one of our weekly brain exercises should involve a game or a puzzle—something that challenges our thinking and requires us to solve a problem . . . and even acquire new information. I'll guide you through some of the most effective brain-boosters.

`Tip:` *Think about your own mind.* Is it active or on autopilot? Are you absorbing new information every day? Are you challenging your brain?

✓ Brain-Booster No. 2: Rev Up Energy and Self-Esteem

I'll show you how to tone your body as you boost your brain. A daily memory regimen in tandem with physical exercise can transform our minds, our bodies, and our overall health. The more we exercise our bodies and our minds, the more we're able to think clearly, feel alert and energetic, and have a markedly increased sense of well-being.

`Tip:` *Think about what gives you a sense of well-being.* Is your goal *homeostasis*—balance? Is the mind-body-emotions connection in balance in your own life?

✓ Brain-Booster No. 3: Pinpoint Hidden Motives

We'll mix deception-detection techniques with Emotional Intelligence for a powerful way to read, relate to, and improve your connections with people—both loved ones and strangers alike. Those who work in people professions will find this information helpful, especially teaching, law enforcement, human resources, and sales.

Tip: *Think about the hidden messages our bodies communicate.* As you examine nonverbal language—behaviors such as posture shifts, gaze aversion, and foot and hand movements—what do you learn?

✓ Brain-Booster No. 4: Build Better Relationships

Having the ability to identify and manage the emotional state in others, as well as the ability to effectively manage and control our own thoughts, can improve our interpersonal relationships. And that's what we will explore. I have combined these abilities with the skills I've learned as a mentalist, not to mention key aspects of deception detection.

Tip: *Think about key relationships in your life.* Identify what works, as well as areas that need improvement. Trust? Communication? Empathy?

✓ Brain-Booster No. 5: Increase Creativity and Intuition

In order to improve our brains, and ultimately our lives, we must change the way we think. I'll show you how to clear away negativity with what I call Memitation techniques. You'll learn to think creatively and boundlessly, and you'll begin to see the world the way our greatest minds have seen it.

Tip: *Think about what sparks creativity in your life.* Who inspires you most? A friend, a teacher . . . a great thinker from the past? What can you learn from this person?

Part One

✦

A BETTER MIND
AT *ANY* AGE

1

Your Brain Can Improve
(I'm Living Proof)

Three Secrets That Changed My Life

I stepped onto the stage at a Connecticut university and decided to shock the audience a bit. I pulled a cinder block out of a bag and held it high in the air.

"I once broke one of these over my head just to impress a girl," I said to the packed crowd of college students, families, and forty-something folks. "Not too smart, right? I mean, a block this heavy could cause some serious head trauma."

I continued talking about the dumb things we do for attention, and just as I got to the punch line of my story, I lobbed the cinder block at a student in the front row.

WHACK! It slammed into his shoulder . . . and then bounced to the ground.

The audience gasped and collectively leapt back in their seats. A few people screamed. My target, a young man who attended the school, was completely stunned.

But the second he started laughing, everyone caught on that the impressively realistic cinder block was actually made out of rubber. It was a harmless prank!

Smiles and relief returned to the audience's faces too.

"Your mind tricked you," I said. "Is seeing really believing? Is perception reality? Maybe we have to view a situation from a different perspective—so we can see the world as it really is. Maybe we need to improve our thinking altogether, so we can have a stronger, more powerful brain."

Right from the start, everyone clued in that my presentation demanded participation, and that it couldn't merely be watched. With each trick and demonstration, I called up different volunteers from the audience, constantly searching for skeptics to turn into believers. I demonstrated the power of my memory, pulled a few pranks on people, and emphasized that as we improve our minds, we ultimately improve our lives.

"As we begin to think creatively and boundlessly," I said, "we'll begin to see the world the way some of greatest minds have seen it. You and I can learn anything we want, and it's surprising how powerful our brains can become when we figure out how to learn."

One of my routines left half the room utterly baffled.

I chose a young lady from the audience and asked her to imagine that she was holding a deck of cards in her hands. Then I asked her to shuffle these pretend cards, choose one, and then put it back into the deck upside down. I wanted it to face the opposite direction of all the other cards. (Again, keep in mind that she wasn't actually holding any cards—they were make-believe.)

"Okay," I said, "so I want you to think about that imaginary card that's upside-down in your imaginary deck. Focus on it for a second. Are you picturing it?"

"Yes," she answered. "I can see it clearly in my mind."

"Great! Now hold that thought."

I then pulled out a real deck of cards, and when I spread them out, only one was facing the opposite direction. I held it up.

"Does this look familiar?" I asked.

The girl's mouth dropped open. "No way," she said. "How did you do that?"

"Was that the card you chose from your imaginary deck?"

The girl nodded *yes*. The crowd roared.

Along with a wide range of other tricks, I also pulled some pranks on the audience while they were in the grip of disbelief.

In one such prank, I explained that I would show an audience member how to cut the cord to one of the microphones and then tie it back together so that it could start working again. Once the audience member completed the knot, I tested the microphone until it came back on.

I then pulled the cord out of the microphone and said, "It's a wireless microphone. You're not doing it," to the surprise and delight of the audience.

In between all of my various card tricks, I demonstrated my ability to memorize virtually anything. "Give me a date in any year back to 1900," I said. "I can recite the day of the week."

I had nearly every zip code in the United States memorized. "Are you from Texas, New York, or Tennessee? I know your zip code. I promise."

Upon entering the theater, each audience member was given a ticket with a serial number, a country, that country's capital city, and a movie title. I instructed everyone to pull out their tickets.

"Give me any piece of information from the ticket," I said. "I'll be able to give every detail of what's on it."

I even offered one hundred dollars to anyone whose ticket stumped me. Nobody went home a hundred dollars richer.

"Sometimes this memory thing scares the crap out of me," I admitted. "My brain is becoming more powerful every day. I think it's knowing a thousand digits of pi that scares me the most—yet it's just so easy for me to remember it!"

And with that, I began rattling off hundreds of those digits.

I ended with encouraging words for every man and woman in that room—especially for those who desired to sharpen their thinking and regain their mental edge: "Everything we need to grow and thrive is right inside our heads," I said. "By its very design, the human brain holds incredible potential for memory, learning, and creativity. Yours and mine do too—far more than we may think."

THREE SECRETS THAT CHANGED MY LIFE

I know from firsthand experience that radical life transformation happens when we sharpen our thinking and regain our mental edge. After employing daily memory-improvement techniques coupled with lifestyle changes—clearing away stress and stepping up my exercise regimen—I grew from an unmotivated Pennsylvania steelworker to what medical experts describe as a "memory phenom," not to mention an in-demand *motivational* speaker. Imagine that! And today brain experts say I possess one of the greatest long-term memories ever documented. Medical doctors are equally baffled when they discover that past health issues are now completely gone!

I had to bust the myths that held me back and replace my thinking with three powerful truths—secrets that have enabled me to thrive in life, not just survive.

Myth-Buster: "I'm Not Smart Enough"

→ *Truth: My Brain Can Improve*

The human brain is the most important organ in the human body—complex, specialized, and mysterious. It's also one of the most hardworking. As the center of reasoning, intellect, memory, consciousness, and emotions, it requires constant nourishment, blood, and oxygen to fuel its many activities.

Proper communication between our brain cells is all wonderfully complex and vitally essential to our sanity. Normal human emotions are determined by whether chemical messengers called neurotransmitters are successful in communicating their messages to our brain cells. On a typical day in the life of our brain, literally trillions of messages are sent and received by these neurotransmitters.[5]

Yep—our brains are a hotbed of activity, and to keep them functioning well, they need our attention. *Memory Magic* lays out a commonsense plan for boosting brain power, beginning with these two crucial steps.

Clear Away Stress

Stress is simply unavoidable, especially in our fast-paced world. But prolonged battles with anxiety, fear, and worry can block our thinking and take a toll on our health. Stress is a big factor in forgetfulness, lack of focus, and an inability to concentrate.

So what can we do? First, clue in to what's going on in our brains.

Two hormones play a big role in triggering and relieving stress: GABA (gamma-aminobutyric acid), what medical doctors call a "happy messenger," and cortisol, what they call a "sad messenger."[6] We need both types of neurotransmitters to coexist and work in tandem inside our brains. When we're ill, sad messengers tell the body to rest. When our lives are endangered, they act as lifesavers, sending our bodies into action to prevent harm. Likewise, happy messengers help us to cope with pain and remain tranquil; they energize us and make us feel vital and optimistic.

So our goal is homeostasis—what medical doctors describe as "the state of metabolic equilibrium between the stimulating and the tranquilizing chemical forces in our bodies." That's a long-winded way of saying "We need to reclaim balance." The question is, *how?* Once we're in an anxious state, how can we get our bodies to return to normal? How can we calm things down? Answer: *Stress management, not stress elimination.* This means taking steps to help our brains activate the relaxation response. I offer detailed steps in my Memory Magic Plan. (You'll find that discussion in Chapter 10—"Brain-Booster No. 5: Increase Creativity and Intuition.")

Clear Away Negativity

Twenty years ago, I was a depressed steelworker in Allentown, Pennsylvania. I was broke, stuck, stressed, and sick. My blood pressure was sky high, and my heart health was quickly sliding downhill, and my brain was entangled in a web of negative thinking. I'd go about my day, constantly ruminating about my circumstances, endangering my health, jeopardizing relationships—and having a miserable time in the process.

But one day, I woke up.

With the support of my wife, my family, and some trusted medical professionals, I took that first step out of my brain fog and toward a radical new life. It began within my mind: clearing away stress, which meant clearing away negativity. In order to improve our brains, and ultimately our lives, we must change the way we think.

Consider these eye-opening insights from my friend Dr. Daniel G. Amen:

> Thoughts are very powerful. They can make your mind and your body feel good, or they can make you feel bad. Every cell in your body is affected by every thought you have. That is why when people get emotionally upset, they frequently develop physical symptoms, such as headaches or stomach-aches. Some physicians think that people who have a lot of negative thoughts are more likely to get cancer. If you can think about good things, you will feel better. . . . You can train your thoughts to be positive and hopeful, or you can allow them to be negative and upset you. . . . One way to learn how to change your thoughts is to notice them when they are negative and talk back to them. When you just think a negative thought without challenging it, your mind believes it and your body reacts to it. When you correct negative thoughts, you take away their power over you.[7]

So much anxiety in our lives is caused by self-condemning thoughts. Whether we realize it or not, we wrongfully judge our-selves. Sometimes a thought enters my mind that triggers fear and worry, and then right away I start thinking, *What's wrong with me?* And then that voice of judgment begins to spiral me downward. Thankfully, I have discovered that I can change the direction of my thoughts. It really is about a choice; it's about getting to a mental place where we are aware of our thoughts—metacognition—so that we can stop them in their tracks. We *can* shift our thinking to what is more peaceful and constructive.

Twenty years ago—as I began to refocus my thoughts and break a destructive cycle of stress and negativity—I gradually learned how to sharpen my thinking, find clarity, and regain my mental edge. (Much more about this in the next chapter.)

But as I headed down a path to a more powerful mind, I discovered that I needed to improve my body, as well. Remember the mind-body-emotions connection?

I needed to treat my *entire* body.

Myth-Buster: "I'm Too Weak"

→ *Truth: My Health Can Improve*

As I get my muscles moving and my heart pumping through exercise, I begin to feel better—almost right away. And after a vigorous workout, my mind is recharged too.

Exercise increases the amount of oxygen available to the brain by making the heart stronger and able to pump more oxygenated blood. That's not the only benefit. My daily workouts create a natural high. I'm not kidding! Exercise stimulates the release of endorphins, neurochemicals that actually have an opiatelike effect on my brain, which is a serious stress-reliever. And speaking of stress relief . . .

Mixed with a daily exercise regimen is time spent stretching and deep breathing. The subtle, invigorating feeling of stretching allows me to get in touch with my muscles. It relaxes my mind and tunes up my body. Likewise, deep breathing quiets my mind and calms my emotions. I take long, steady breaths from the diaphragm. This slows down my heart rate, lowers my blood pressure, and helps my body use oxygen more efficiently. Not only do our lungs supply red blood cells with fresh oxygen—enabling normal cell function and proper metabolism—they also rid our bodies of harmful waste products such as carbon dioxide.

So stretching and deep breathing enable me to clear away stress and negativity, which results in greater clarity and intuition. But it's a daily exercise regimen that improves everything. And when I say *exercise*, I don't just mean our muscles. I mean our brains too. Lots more on that very soon.

Exercise Your Body

Our bodies are meant to be active. The harder we work them and the better the nutrients we put into them, the leaner, stronger, and more energetic they will become. In fact, the chemicals produced during moderate exercise can enhance the function of the immune system and train our bodies to deal with stress under controlled circumstances.

Here are the two types of exercise that we need to incorporate into our daily lives:

Aerobic Activity. The technical definition is "training with oxygen." In other words, an activity that gets your heart pumping and air flowing through your body: walking, hiking, jogging, swimming, bicycling, or cross-country skiing. The benefits are indisputable:

- It strengthens our hearts
- It lowers our blood pressure
- It improves metabolism
- 20–30 minutes of sustained activity starts burning off fat stores
- It releases endorphins and other "feel-good" hormones

Anaerobic Exercise. This means "training without oxygen," and it involves all forms of high-intensity activity that are engaged for short periods of time. Examples include sprinting, resistance training (working out with weights), powerlifting, tennis, racquetball . . . and any other sport you can think of that causes fatigue to the muscles with harder but shorter bursts of energy. During anaerobic exercise, our cardiovascular system has a challenging time delivering the necessary levels of oxygen to our muscles fast enough. And since muscles require air to maintain prolonged exertion, anaerobic exercises can only continue for short periods of time. Why is it important for overall good health? Resistance training, for example, provides these benefits:

+ It improves muscle strength, which enhances other athletic pursuits
+ It builds and maintains a lean, toned body
+ It enhances weight loss
+ It helps us fight stress through vigorous exercise

As we get our bodies moving, we've got to stimulate our minds, as well.

Exercise Your Brain

Brain cells communicate with one another through tiny branchlike cells called dendrites. I don't mean to be the bearer of bad news, but as we age, our ability to form dendrites declines, which is why our memory wanes and we have more difficulty learning new tasks. Through the years there is a constant "brain drain," resulting in fewer and fewer new dendrites.

But again, there's no need to throw in the towel and settle for the beige walls of the nursing home! Dr. Amen and his colleagues have learned that the brain is extremely resilient and that it has an amazing capacity to restore itself if it is given the proper stimulation.

In fact, if we use our brains by challenging ourselves mentally, we can build new nerve connections and strengthen neuron pathways. The result: increased brain power and a more youthful functioning brain. What are some ways that we can pump those neurons?

+ Play a brain game or solve a puzzle weekly
+ Challenge our minds by engaging in new mental tasks
+ Learn new facts and feed our brains with information every day
+ Turn off the TV and read
+ Stimulate our brains with daily social interaction

The more I exercise my body and my brain, the more I'm able to think clearly, I feel alert and energetic, and I have a markedly increased sense of well-being. Again, we'll go into much more detail in Part Two. For example, in Chapter 5, I'll introduce you to my powerful brain-improvement program—what I call Cogmental Intelligence. We'll continue the discussion in Chapter 6, where we'll explore my favorite brain games that will give your gray matter a good workout. In Chapter 7, we'll go deeper into the body-mind-emotions connection with a stress-relieving, body-toning program.

Myth-Buster: "I'm Too Old"

→ *Truth: My Quality of Life Can Improve*

As I mentioned earlier, brain cells communicate with one another through dendrites. The growth of these cells peaks before adolescence, which is one of the reasons that children have the ability to pick up languages, musical instruments, and other skills while adults struggle with them.[8]

The bad news: As we age, our ability to form dendrites declines and brain drain sets in. The good news: We can take the steps right now to improve our minds and increase our brain power. It's never too late, and we're never too old to make some positive changes.

But in spite of slick advertising campaigns, there isn't an easy pill that can give us instant results. We simply can't continue our soft lifestyle as couch potatoes and expect our brains to improve. We have to change our thinking and put forth the effort.

I'm in my sixties, and I'm in the best shape ever—both mentally and physically. In addition to taking the steps I've outlined in this chapter, there's one more secret I have discovered: Nothing is stopping any of us from improving our quality of life. The sad fact is, we are our own worst enemies. We limit ourselves and block all the possibilities before us. Yet grasping these next two truths can give us the motivational fuel we need to improve.

Learn to Think Creatively

Every one of us was born with the potential for greatness. Even if we have yet to revolutionize anyone's ideas about the planet or its inhabitants, we came into the world with the same spark of genius we see in some of history's greatest minds both past and present: Nicolaus Copernicus, Leonardo da Vinci, Marie Curie, Jane Austen, Pablo Picasso, Albert Einstein, Martin Luther King, Shirley Ann Jackson, Mae C. Jemison.[9]

What did these men and women have in common? They each were able to think outside the box; to think creatively and limitlessly in order to harness their minds' power. But the secret to their success was their intuitive understanding of *how* to learn.

You and I can learn anything we want, and it's surprising how powerful our brains can become when we figure out how to learn. Everything we need to grow and thrive is right inside our heads, and by its very design, the human brain holds incredible potential for memory, learning, and creativity. Yours and mine do too—far more than we may think.

The 100-billion neuron tally is a simple fact of human physiology, according to the great neurologist Sir Charles Sherrington, who described the human brain as "an enchanted loom" ready to weave a unique tapestry of creative self-expression.[10]

But the power of our minds can be unlocked only with the knowledge of how to develop that potential, and the will to put those hundreds of billions of fact-learning, connection-building neurons to work in the most effective, creative ways possible.[11]

This is exactly what my Memory Magic Plan and Cogmental Intelligence training can help you to achieve. In the days ahead, you'll learn how to unleash your creativity and maximize your mental abilities.

Learn to Think Boundlessly

Whether we do it out of fear, insecurity, wounds from the past, or negativity, we limit ourselves with two destructive words: "I can't."

"I can't because I'm too old."

"I can't because I'm just not smart enough."

"I can't because I'm afraid I'll fail."

I once thought this way. There was a time when I tucked my life into a tiny box and put up all kinds of mental barriers around it, ensuring that I'd never crawl out. *I am who I am*, I reasoned. *I'm ordinary—nobody of significance who has anything worthwhile to contribute to the world.* Speak in front of thousands of people, become friends with celebrities, appear on national TV, and write a book?! These things seemed like impossibilities for a simple Pennsylvania steelworker. Hitting age sixty just seemed to seal the deal.

I am who I am. I can't learn anything new, I can't change, I can't improve my life.

It's time to remove "I can't" from our mind-set. It's time to think boundlessly . . . and to start achieving what we never, ever thought we could accomplish. With practical physical and mental exercises, I'll guide you using breakthrough thinking principles that can help you sharpen your edge for real-world results.

As you begin to think creatively and boundlessly, you'll begin to see the world the way some of the greatest minds have seen it. Here's how Martin Kemp, Professor of the History of Art at the University of Oxford, defines the thought process of a brilliant mind. He describes a way of thinking that isn't out of reach for you and me:

> Through some magnificent act of insight, intuition, inspiration, brain wave, conviction, whatever we might call it, the genius sees or senses something from a different perspective. Their new perspective provides a view that ultimately proves so compelling that we can never see things in quite the same way again. What they see is often a bigger picture than we can readily grasp. And they can do this because they sense how the parts fit into the whole, the deeper harmonic resonance of things that may seem on the surface to be unrelated.[12]

✦

Today, my "better mind, better life" message is resonating with people from all walks of life—everyone from Hollywood actors and pro athletes to Ivy League academics and ordinary folks alike. Each year, I crisscross the globe, speaking in a wide range of venues: corporate retreats, medical symposiums, MIT conferences, the Pentagon, the USO Entertainment Tour, Wounded Warrior

Project events, memory competitions, and much more. In addition, my abilities as a mentalist have impressed millions on *The Tonight Show*, *The Ellen DeGeneres Show*, *Today*, and *The Howard Stern Show*. I was also selected by NBC as one of the top-ten mentalists in the world and invited to compete nationally on the network's live reality show called *Phenomenon*.

That word—*phenomenon*—once seemed so out of reach for me. I was far from it, yet now I'm doing things that boggle my mind. Today I can memorize a shuffled deck of cards in less than a minute, share thousands of digits of pi, and recite facts from sports almanacs, medical journals, and the Scrabble dictionary.

My once-sick body is now healthy, and my mind continues to grow stronger every day. My program can help you too. Let's get started!

2

Myth-Buster:
"I'm Not Smart Enough"

*My Journey from Unmotivated Steelworker
to Memory Expert*

It was now spring of 2007 and within a three-week span, I'd crisscrossed the country on a hectic travel schedule—speaking to kids, college students, business professionals, and military veterans alike. My talks ranged from memory to mentalism, and at each venue, I entertained crowds with card tricks and feats of magic. Between shows, I conducted back-to-back interviews with the media, shook a lot of hands, and met thousands of interesting people from all walks of life.

But finally, the mad push was over and at this very moment, I was in my absolute happy place: lying in bed next to my wife, Lynn—my best friend!

It didn't matter that the first rays of sunlight were breaking through the slits in our window shade, reminding us that it was morning again ... *Monday morning.* Lynn and I were gearing up for a week of much-needed R&R, and the possibilities were endless: afternoon movie marathons, walks in the park, bike rides, snuggle time with the grandkids, dinner at our favorite hangout—

That's when it happened. RING!

The piercing shrill of my cell phone shattered all those happy thoughts. "Ignore it," I insisted. "So, Lynn, I was thinking maybe we could head into the city . . . or take a long drive to the beach—"

RI-I-I-NG! RI-I-I-NG!

"Are you going to get that or what?" Lynn asked.

"Just let it go, okay? This is our week."

RI-I-I-NG! RI-I-I-NG! RI-I-I-NG!

"It's driving me crazy," my wife said, with a hint of annoyance in her voice.

I yanked the phone off my nightstand and punched the on button. "Bet it's another job," I said under my breath.

I was quickly greeted by an unfamiliar voice—a man who introduced himself as the principal of an Allentown, Pennsylvania, high school. "Yep, it's another gig," I whispered to Lynn. But little did I realize this show was going to be way different from anything I'd ever done. I was about to receive a very special invitation to "pay it forward."

"Mr. Karol," the man said, "I've heard all about your reputation for having a powerful memory—and how you use it to motivate others. So I was wondering if . . . well, what I'm trying to say is, it would mean the world to my teachers and my school if you could—"

The principal eventually coughed out his request. He explained that he was desperately trying to reach some at-risk students who were about to repeat a hopeless cycle of drugs, crime, violence, and poverty. Specifically, he was worried about twenty-two ninth graders who were on the verge of flunking out of school. He needed someone to spend an afternoon motivating them—ultimately getting these kids excited about learning.

"You are the right person for the job," the school administrator said to me. "These students don't have to become tragic statistics. Each one of them is a sharp kid with so much untapped potential. The crazy thing is, they've been labeled *losers*, and so they're making every effort to live up to their reputations."

I leaned back on my pillow and nodded my head in agreement. His words hit a nerve inside, and my own childhood memories began flooding my mind: images of pain and bullying. I knew exactly what these kids were going through, because I was once just like them.

"YES!" I told the principal, without knowing all the details. "Count me in. In fact, I'm available as early as this Thursday."

I glanced at my wife. She just smiled and gave me a wink. She knew I couldn't stay away for long from my other happy place: helping people realize that a stronger mind is within reach—and a stronger mind changes everything.

✦

I was introduced as a man who had one of the greatest long-term memories ever documented; a memory champion who baffled MIT scientists and Pentagon elites. "Jim Karol is not one in a million," the principal said, quoting the medical community. "He's not one in a billion. Jim is one on the planet!" He then invited the students to put their hands together and welcome "a mentalist, a magician, and a world-class deception detector."

But when I stepped in front of the group, I'm sure they thought I looked more like a biker than a brainiac! I was decked out in a black leather jacket, a black tee, and sunglasses.

I scanned the crowd with one goal in mind: Reach these kids. I needed to break through the age barrier and find a way to connect with them. They simply couldn't think of me as a crazy old guy. My approach was similar to the one I took with veterans—guys and ladies who battled PTSD. This group would spend day after day with professionals who wore white jackets and carried clipboards. They spoke only one language: medical-ese. But every time I greeted the vets—looking more like a biker—I instantly had their attention. And the second I'd show them card tricks, I'd break down the barriers and engage their senses.

I'd hoped to have the same rapport with this group.

So the first thing I said was, "Have any of you ever seen the movie *Jack-a-s-s Number Two*?" (I spelled out the movie title, because I didn't have the heart to cuss in front of kids!)

Hands popped up all over the room.

"I bet you didn't know this about me," I said, "but I made a cameo appearance in the movie."

Suddenly, this really big kid with massive piercings—and tons of attitude—slumped back in his seat, folded his arms, and blurted, "Yeah, right. I don't think so!"

But just at that moment, another student who recognized me got excited and yelled, "Oh, man . . . Jim Karol was in the movie. He's the guy who threw playing cards at a character named Wee-Man. It really is you!"

I won't go into the details of *where* I threw those cards or the effect this stunt had on Wee-Man, but I will say this: The movie is filled with gross stunts and "boy humor." (I think you get the picture.)

At that moment, I had all these kids eating out of my hand— all because I had made an appearance in one of the *Jackass* movies. But that's what you have to do when it comes to relationships with people—at home, at school, and in the workplace. In order to be heard by various groups, we have to win them over and gain their trust. We have to find their "It factor"—the thing that grabs their attention so we can make a connection. If this doesn't happen, they're not going to listen—regardless of their age. (More on this in Chapters 8 and 9.)

I thought to myself, *Okay—now that I have them, I need to do something way cool in order to get them excited about learning.*

So I showed them trick after trick, and then I blew them away with demonstrations on the power of the human mind. Little by little, I tied in educational techniques.

And then I paused, turned to the crowd, and said, "How many of you are flunking math?"

A couple of hands went up. Next question: "How many are flunking history?"

Just about every hand went up. I instantly knew the direction to take the remainder of my presentation. So on the fly, I decided to do something with U.S. presidents.

"Let me show you a memory technique that you can learn today," I said. "When I was your age, I had to learn the names of every president—from Washington to the current one at the time."

At that point, I raced through forty-three names practically without taking a breath. As the words flew out of my mouth, I scanned the crowd. The kids were really into it. Eyes grew wide and giant smiles stretched across otherwise skeptical, cynical faces. So here I was—a rough-looking guy from a *Jackass* movie—rattling off names like a college professor. Once I spit out the last president's name, I stepped up to the chalkboard and scribbled a memory system—specifically, a visual link method and a rhyming peg (more about this in Chapter 6)—and I demonstrated how to memorize the first ten names: Washington, Adams, Jefferson, Madison, Monroe, Adams, Jackson, Van Buren, Harrison, Tyler.

Once I wrote out a memory trick for the first ten presidents, I said, "I need volunteers to come up here and write out a memory plan for the next ten, and the ten after that . . . all the way to our current president."

Kids were falling out of their chairs to volunteer. They were laughing—and having fun *learning*. These so-called hardened students were anything but thugs or lost causes . . . or any of the other derogatory words that had been slapped on them. And deep inside, I was cheering them on. (So many hurtful words had once been slapped on *me* when I was a kid.)

I wrapped up my presentation with another card trick, and then I held up a DVD that was available at the time: *Jim Karol's Cool Card Tricks*. "The secret to this trick is revealed right here," I told the students. "And I want you to have a free copy, but you have to earn it. Here's how: Memorize the presidents tonight, using the technique I showed you. Come back tomorrow and recite the list flawlessly to your principal, and he'll give you your very own copy."

The principal joined me up front and sweetened the deal: "Not only will you get Jim's DVD," he said, "but if you can recite the presidents, I'll take you to the Yankee Stadium to see a game! You can even bring your parents or guardians."

Suddenly, everyone in the room was walking on clouds. They were high-fiving me as they headed out the door, promising that they were going to meet the challenge.

And that's exactly what they did!

The next morning, I received a phone call from the principal. "Hey, do you have twenty-two of those DVDs?" he asked.

"What?" I laughed. "You're kidding me!"

"It's no joke," he said. "They did it—and you helped them. The kids filed into my office one by one . . . each reciting the presidents of the United States. You gave them confidence and opened their eyes to something better. And that's exactly what they needed."

Here's the best part of the story: Every one of these students went on to graduate from high school. They got excited about learning, which ultimately changed their lives.

Unlocking Ultimate Opportunities

Like I said, I was once just like these kids. Spending an afternoon with them took me back to my high school days. It also confirmed something else that I've observed through the years: Motivation and memory go hand in hand.

We study and memorize the things that excite us. But in order to master a topic—and lock it into our long-term memory—we need the right kind of motivation to move us forward. For the teens, the promise of a reward (the DVD and the trip to the Yankees game) gave them the fuel to learn something new. For each one of us, that motivation takes on so many different forms: bragging rights, affirmation from our peers, a paycheck . . . even a diploma.

But during my childhood, my life desperately fell short in the motivation department. I struggled with grades, relationships . . . and especially with bullies. I was pushed around by both kids *and* teachers, and I was constantly made fun of. Day after day, the second I'd set foot in my school campus, and the word bullets would fly.

The crazy thing is, I had MIT- or Harvard-level potential, yet—just like that group of ninth graders—I was fooled by the labels people slapped on me. I believed all the lies I was told and made every effort to live up to my reputation of being a loser. I was shy and backward. I mean really shy. I couldn't even look people in the eye. And it seemed that the older I got, the more I became bullied. When I was in high school, constant bullying plunged my grades from Cs and Ds to Fs. (I think I was the first kid to ever get an F minus!) I flunked my senior year, and had to attend summer school in order to get my diploma.

After high school, my circumstances didn't change much. I got a job in Allentown, Pennsylvania, as a steelworker . . . only to be pushed around on the factory floor. (You'll read more about this in the next chapter.) There didn't seem to be anything remarkable about my life—and if I believed all the ugly labels people slapped on me, I didn't have much to hope for either. I just wasn't smart enough . . . or so I thought.

In spite of my rough childhood and rocky young adult years, I had a head full of dreams and a heart filled with passion. Deep inside, I knew my life could be better. Eventually, I learned that improving my brain was the first step toward improving my life. And guess what? Change is possible for every man and woman—regardless of our age and our circumstances.

Regardless of where I speak and who I talk to, I want everyone to grasp three truths:

1. Our minds are powerful.
2. Our own potential for a stronger memory can improve our health, our relationships, our careers, and our overall quality of life.
3. A better memory is within reach.

The way I turn skeptics into believers is through my own story.

Before we explore some of those dreams and truths that changed my life, let's rewind my story a bit, and take a peek at some of the childhood pain I experienced. Here's a scene from my awkward teen years that began to define my thinking. Constant bullying weakened my self-confidence.

Shot Down by Word Bullets

I swung open the cafeteria doors, scanned the room, and then froze. A sharp, sickening pain jabbed at the pit of my stomach.

Day after day, the same thing, I thought. *I just can't handle this anymore.*

It wasn't the strange cafeteria smells that made me queasy. I knew I was about to face something far worse: the firing squad at the *cool kids' table.*

"Oh look who it is," blurted a sarcastic voice. "It's our best friend, Jim. Come sit here, Jim—we've been waiting for you!"

My heart began playing keyboards with my rib cage, and every muscle grew tense. I took a deep breath and stepped into the food line. Suddenly the same, worn-out barrage of painful word bullets began to fly.

"Dork."

"Wimp."

"Loser."

An empty milk carton smacked me on the side of my head, and laughter rose from the table. I squeezed shut my eyes.

Why does this stupid line have to go past these guys? I asked myself. *And why won't they leave me alone?*

It got to a point where the few friends I had wouldn't even sit by me during lunch. We'd get to the cafeteria, and they'd conveniently disappear.

So why did some of the guys at school give me such a hard time? I was awkward and struggled to hold a conversation with others. I couldn't even look people in the eye.

By the end of my high school years, my grades had slipped and I'd begun to believe all the hateful things people said about me.

Little by little, I pulled away from others—kids and adults alike—and I became more of an introvert.

How Negative Words Can Define Us

Words can be cruel.

In fact, they can hurt . . . even destroy.

Unlike a gunshot or knife wound, reckless words can weaken a person's self-confidence. This includes those seemingly innocent cuts, slams, and jabs; those playful—but unkind and unflattering—labels we like to pin on others. We use them at school, in the workplace, in our families, and all throughout our communities. But the wounds caused by reckless words often don't heal for many years, if ever. They enter our ears and burrow themselves deep into our hearts. They may be stored deep in the mind, but they are never completely forgotten.

I was a prime example.

When I became an adult, here's what I learned about bullying and negativity: Children who are subjected to bullying or who are brought up in an atmosphere where harsh criticism, taunts, and mocking are part of their daily routine can—and will—easily internalize the messages behind the words. If they are constantly told that they are slow, dumb, and aren't worth very much, they'll begin to believe it.

Hey, if the adults around me think I'm a loser, it must be true.

Even worse, they may end up repeating the cycle. Cruelty breeds cruelty. A child who knows nothing else but mockery, name calling, and sarcasm may end up becoming a bully.[13] The effects caused by negative words, if that's all a child knows, are long-lasting and far-reaching.

We need to think hard about the words we use—at home, at school, and at work. What we say, and how we say it, can change a life forever, and not for the good. There are a lot of broken people in this world. I'd say that *all* are broken, but only a few admit it. We like to believe we're okay, that we have it all together; it makes us feel better about ourselves.

I've learned that it's okay to be broken. When we get to this point, we can put away all the junk that gets in the way—and move on toward healing. Thankfully, I didn't let all those cruel words define me. I was able to escape the negativity and change my life.

✦

Just as my teenage years hit rock bottom, I desperately needed to bust a myth (I'm just not smart enough) and grasp a truth (my brain can improve). What would help me out of my rut so I could change my life? You'll find the answers in the next chapter!

I'm sorry to leave you with a cliff-hanger, but first, I want to spill the beans a bit and give you three truths that eventually got my feet (and brain) moving in the right direction; truths that I want you to grasp . . .

Truth #1: Our Minds Are Powerful

We know that the human brain is a powerful organ, but many of us aren't aware of how much the mind is truly capable of and how much *more* powerful it can become as we learn. By exercising the brain—regardless of our IQ—we can achieve what we never thought was possible.

A few years back, as I was reading about the power of the brain, I came across an eye-opening article in *Scientific American*. I nearly fell out of my chair when I read the bio of the author. It wasn't a leading scientist or a brain surgeon. The author was a seventeen-year-old student named Ken Gu. Suddenly, the magazine had my attention.

This future mover and shaker was fascinated with learning and how the brain works, so he did his homework and he found a unique way of sharing his findings. He entered his writing in a contest hosted by the magazine and ended up getting his work published.

I thought, *How perfect! This young thinker who the world would never label an expert—someone who has so much yet to learn—so beautifully demonstrates the power of the mind.*

I firmly believe that each one of us has the potential to accomplish anything we put our mind to. We must shed the barriers that hold us back—whether it's past bullying and negativity or the myth that we aren't smart enough—and get our feet (and our brains) moving forward.

Here are highlights of what the young man wrote:

[The brain] has a massive capacity of around 2.5 petabytes. . . . In case that sounds out of context for you, I'll put it into gigabytes, the larger storage unit used on most phones. The average brain can hold 2,500,000 gigabytes of information. That's equal to 156,250 16GB iPhones. To get even bigger numbers, we can convert this to bits, the 1s and 0s that make up technology itself. To have the memory of the brain on a computer, that computer would need to be able to encode 22,517,998,136,850,000 1s and 0s. That number is 22 quadrillion, 517 trillion, 998 billion, 136 million, 850 thousand. The brain can also do things that nothing else can. It can process senses, control our whole body (except some parts the spinal cord controls including reflex arcs),

JUST HOW POWERFUL IS THE HUMAN BRAIN?

Here are examples of our extremely vast brain capacity:

Bytes

- 1 byte can store 1 character, e.g. *A* or *x* or *$* or 9.1 megabyte is equal to about 1 million bytes of data
- 1,024 megabytes of data equals 1 gigabyte of data
- 1,024 gigabytes of data equals 1 terabyte of data

Terabytes

- The Library of Congress is the largest library in the United States. It features 883 miles of shelf space, containing 164 million items total, including 40 million books
- The entire Library of Congress takes up almost 15 terabytes of data
- 1,024 terabytes of data equals 1 petabyte of data
- The human brain can store up to 2.5 petabytes of data—that's equivalent to 250 Libraries of Congress

and think. The reason we have philosophers, teachers, students, engineers, et cetera is due to the massive power of the brain. To add to the craziness, we have to remind ourselves that this organ that is about 3 pounds (1.3–1.4 kg) on average and has so many parts that came from a single cell in the beginning of life, just makes it even crazier.[14]

Truth #2: A Strong Mind Can Change Everything

The Problem: From aging immune systems and increased stress to decreased memories, a war is being waged inside our bodies. Our joints become arthritic, our bones brittle, our arteries clogged, our lung capacities shrunken, and our muscle strength diminished. And that fog we often feel trapped in is very real. Changes in brain function can interfere with our ability to perform our jobs, pursue our interests, or even engage in social activities.

The Solution: I am living proof that it's never too late and we're never too old to reverse the damage and reclaim our bodies and our minds. Using my memory-boosting system—what I call Cogmental Intelligence—coupled with lifestyle changes, we *can* preserve and even enhance our memory and other aspects of mental function.

Concentration, alertness, and the ability to focus can be strengthened, leading to improvements in problem-solving ability, productivity, and even IQ.

My cutting-edge program shows how we can:

- Sharpen our thinking and regain our mental edge
- Live free from disease
- Get in the best physical shape of our lives
- Clear away negativity and stress
- Become more creative and innovative

Truth #3: A Better Memory Is Within Reach

Following my Memory Magic plan can enable you to . . .

Think creatively and boundlessly—and begin achieving what you never, ever thought you could accomplish. Through practical physical and mental exercises, I'll guide you using thinking and stress-relieving principles that can help you sharpen your edge for real-world results.

Feel healthier, stronger, and more in tune with your life's purpose. The more we exercise our bodies and our minds, the more we're able to think clearly, feel alert and energetic, and have a markedly increased sense of well-being.

Do what some of the world's most brilliant minds have discovered. Great thinkers have learned how to put their hundreds of billions of fact-learning, connection-building neurons to work in the most effective, creative ways possible. As you work your way through the pages of this book, you will learn that nothing is stopping any of us from improving our quality of life. You can experience increased brain power and a more youthful functioning brain, as well as a stronger, healthier body.

LET'S TAKE OUR MINDS TO THE NEXT LEVEL

We are our own worst enemies, limiting ourselves because of poor self-confidence and negativity. (For example, believing that we're just too average to be extraordinary.) Another barrier: Our health is just too far gone.

3

Myth-Buster: "I'm Too Weak"

*How a Daily Memory Regimen Transformed My
Brain, My Body, and My Overall Health*

Living Here in Allentown

The alarm blared at 6:00 a.m. right on cue, and as soon as my feet
hit the floor, I started preparing my brain for what I knew was
ahead: humiliation, put-downs, negativity—the message that my
life was nothing but a joke and that I didn't even deserve the oxygen
I was using up.

"Here I go again," I groaned.

The same thing over and over. Remember the 1993 film *Groundhog Day?* That was my life too—at least for a season.

In the movie, a cynical weatherman named Phil (played by Bill
Murray) was trapped in a personal time warp—the same day in the
same small town of Punxsutawney. His life was filled with tension,
and his thinking was cloudy. He was rude and impulsive, and he
didn't know how to manage his own emotions. At first, Phil saw no
escape—no clear way to change his circumstances.

At the time, I felt just as stuck and every bit as cynical.

I tried going to a community college right out of high school, but that just didn't work out. So I did what everyone else in Allentown did at the time: I took a job at a Pennsylvania steel mill in nearby Bethlehem. (Yep—it was just like the Billy Joel song!)

Ultimately, working in a steel mill became my life. My dad worked there . . . right along with my uncles, cousins, and every other man I knew. And it was a good life, an honorable one. What I didn't realize was how harsh some of the people could be, which explained the stress my dad had to endure.

The mill was filled with plenty of great folks—tattooed Hulks, grizzled old guys, men and women who loved their families—right along with the bottom of the barrel: street fighters, the certifiably insane, and one of the worst bullies I'd ever met. It's no exaggeration to say that this particular guy seemed as if he stepped right out of a prison yard and onto the factory floor. The anguish that he felt from his own lot in life was constantly inflicted on everyone around him—especially on me. (There was definitely a *Shawshank Redemption* vibe going on with him!)

I'll never forget my first day on the job. Since I was the "fresh meat," this guy took pleasure in ripping me to shreds. Even though I grew up in the toughest part of Allentown—the 6th Ward—and in spite of the fact that I thought I'd seen it all, the misery of this specific individual at the mill was worse than anything I'd ever imagined. I remember thinking, *Man, high school was heaven compared with this hell.*

But I eventually fought back . . . and he never bothered me again.

So I settled into my life at the steel mill, and things smoothed out for a while. Soon I met this pretty young lady who lived in Catasauqua, Pennsylvania, just outside of Allentown. She stood just under five feet tall, and her name was Lynn. We started dating and quickly fell in love. I think you can figure out what happened next: We got married, had a couple of babies, and built a really good life together. Lynn and my kids were the bright spots of my life—the greatest blessings of all.

The love and support I received from my family opened my eyes and my heart to all kinds of dreams swirling around in my head. Somewhere along the way, an unexpected interest began to take root inside me: a fascination with magic.

Eventually, I met the owner of a magic shop who was willing to teach me some of the tricks of the trade. I was instantly blown away by his ability to fool the eye and so skillfully pull off various feats of illusion.

This is it, I thought to myself. *I'm going to become a magician, and one day, I'm going to entertain crowds coast to coast!*

The question was, how? I worked in a steel mill.

Day after day, I'd roll into a parking space outside the mill and would just stare at the long line of workers filing in. As I relived my own *Groundhog Day* and steered clear of that *Shawshank* animal, I found myself feeling like yet another nineties movie character: Joe Banks—the discontented factory worker in the movie *Joe Versus the Volcano.*

The passive hypochondriac (played by Tom Hanks) yearned for adventure. More than anything, he wanted a life filled with meaning and purpose. Yet he felt too sick and too stuck to do anything about it. Eventually, after being falsely diagnosed with an imaginary disease—a "brain cloud"—Joe mustered up the courage to flee his pointless existence.

Do I have the courage to change my life too? I wondered. *Or is this it—the best I'll ever be . . . the most I'll ever accomplish?*

Maybe life imitates art, or maybe it's the other way around—I don't know. But just like the anxious character in the movie, it took some unexpected challenges and a real health scare to change my world.

They're Closing All the Factories Down

First, I suffered a knee injury while playing flag football with a bunch of fellow steelworkers.

Second, just to add insult to injury (literally), I got laid off.

So here I was, hobbling around on crutches, collecting unemployment, with a little baby in one arm and another one on the way. (My wife was eight and a half months pregnant.) But we weren't the only ones who were tossed aside by a company that downsized. Back then, half the town was laid off—just as Billy Joel sang in his iconic song.

How on earth can we make ends meet? Magic isn't paying the bills— not yet anyway.

And then it hit me. *I'll do what any other self-respecting husband would do in these circumstances: I'll take over my wife's Avon account.*

So in the days that followed, I went door-to-door selling her products. Can you imagine how strange I must have looked to all those unsuspecting Pennsylvania ladies? They'd peek out their windows and would see a burly ex-steelworker lugging around a case full of makeup and skin-care goods.

"Allow me to introduce myself," I'd say with a cheesy grin. I'd hand them a flyer with my name on it. "I'm your Avon rep."

They'd glance at my handout, and then they'd size me up from head to toe. I would pull out a deck of cards and show them a magic trick or two, and instead of slamming the door in my face, they either felt sorry for me or they liked my card tricks. My sales went through the roof. In fact, I became one of the area's highest-grossing Avon reps. (No kidding!) A large group of Avon reps even hired me to appear at a motivational event and share my story with hundreds of women. When you think about it, that was nothing short of remarkable.

Remember how shy I was as a teen? Remember the backward-ness that held me down at the mill? Magic seemed to cure all that. Impressing others with card tricks built up my self-confidence, and suddenly, I could look people in the eye and actually carry on a conversation.

Of course, the kinds of things I was forced to talk about at this point in my life didn't exactly send chills down my spine: "We're running a two-for-one special on lotions this month," I'd tell the ladies. "Oh, and those colors also come in blush, pink, and bubble-gum."

Here was my favorite line: "I think we have a coupon for that!"

But, hey, at least this script was way better than the one I repeated at the steel mill: "Back off, buddy!"

Months turned into years, and a fresh direction was definitely unfolding for me. But just as the challenges of life are often portrayed in art—remember *Joe Versus the Volcano?*—my path forward would involve another crazy twist and turn . . . and an even bigger surprise.

Like Joe Banks, I had my own "brain cloud" to overcome.

But the Restlessness Was Handed Down

Chest pains sent me to the emergency room.

"I'm afraid I have some difficult news, Mr. Karol," my cardiologist told me. (As if I needed more problems!) "Your heart isn't keeping up a healthy beat, and stress is making matters worse. You've got to make some changes—and you've got to make them now."

More changes? I thought. *Will life smooth out again?*

"You have a condition called cardiomyopathy," he explained. "This is a disease of the heart muscle that makes it harder for this organ to pump blood to the rest of your body. Even though your birth certificate says forty-nine, you've got the heartbeat of a ninety-three-year-old."

In addition to that, the doctor informed me that I had an enlarged heart. At first that sounded good to me because everyone wants a big heart, right? But then I noticed the seriousness in his eyes. "It's called cardiomegaly, and it isn't a disease, but rather a sign of another condition," he explained. "In your case, it's because of stress."

So a combination of genetics, stress, and poor coping skills had finally caught up with me. My mind was clouded by fear and negativity . . . and it was killing my body.

Even though all this bad news was hard to accept, I still managed to find a silver lining: My health scare was the wake-up call I needed to radically transform my life—something I'd been yearning to do. So with the support of Lynn, my kids, and some trusted medical professionals, I embraced a better life.

It began with my body. I was determined to ride my stationary bike every day and cut out all of the junk food I ate. And there's plenty of it in my part of the country, which is just a stone's throw from Philadelphia. Ever try an authentic Philly cheesesteak? Or how about our pizza or bacon grease popcorn? And after meals like these, you have to have a box of chocolate donuts. While my state is the capitol of addicting comfort food, I managed to cut out all of it. My new diet consisted of entrees like grilled chicken and salads . . . and all things heart-healthy.

Next, I focused on my mind. Since rehabbing on a stationary bike is as boring as watching golf on TV or doing your tax returns, I started entertaining myself with a deck of cards. As I pedaled feverishly, I would memorize the order of these cards. Soon, I graduated to more challenging mind exercises, such as learning random facts and figures or memorizing blocks of information like the periodic table of elements—anything to engage my brain.

Finally, I took the steps to clear away stress and negativity. In order to improve our brains, and ultimately our lives, we must change the way we think. For example, positive attitudes and thoughts promote healing and well-being, while negativity actually blocks creativity and intuition.

After just a few months of moving my body, engaging my mind, and managing stress, my energy and mental abilities began to soar. Essentially, I gave my brain a workout as I exercised my body. This step alone is one of the biggest secrets to skyrocketing our memory, and the results can be amazing. Here's what happens: Feeding our minds information while doing physical exercise increases blood flow to our brains *and* increases nitric oxide levels. Our bodies naturally produce this molecule, which relaxes the inner muscles of the blood vessels, causing them to widen and increase circulation. Blood, nutrients, and oxygen travel throughout our bodies more effectively and efficiently. Hence, we feel better and think better too.

Research has proved that consistent, daily exercise increases antioxidant activity, and it helps to reduce the breakdown of nitric oxide caused by free radicals. Here are two other benefits of my dual approach to exercise:

(1) We become more energized.

(2) We are able to increase mental challenges.

At one point, I was able to memorize a hundred digits of pi a day. While this may sound like a bunch of useless information, engaging my brain in this way actually improved how it functioned, enabling it to grow and making it more powerful. In fact, my knowledge began to double and triple.

I like to think that my story has been somewhat interesting so far—if not downright strange. But just wait until you read the next scene. If you're not yet convinced that my Memory Magic plan can help you, I hope this changes your mind.

It's Hard to Keep a Good Man Down

Ten years had sped by, and I was a changed man. I'd sworn off Philly cheesesteaks and had hardly ever gone off the wagon. Like I said, I cheated maybe once or twice. And now at age fifty-nine, I needed to renew my life insurance, so I visited my doctor for a physical.

My medical professional reviewed my records, groaned a few times, shook his head endlessly, and then let out a deep sigh. "I'm sorry to tell you this, but because of the cardiomyopathy, it's going to be next to impossible to get insurance."

I thought to myself, *I don't think I even have that anymore.*

"Could you test me anyway, Doc," I insisted. "I feel pretty good, and I think I'm a different man now."

"Well you certainly look good," the doctor said. "But your medical history—yikes!"

He looked at me like I was crazy, but conceded anyway. The testing, probing, and prodding commenced, and then the doctor sat down on his stool and gasped.

"You've got to be kidding me," he said.

"Is everything okay?" I asked.

"Way better than okay," he said. "I want to know what on earth you've been doing. You look younger than you did ten years ago—and your heart has proven that too."

I told him the whole story about the bike, the energy, the whole thing—especially the diet. He started giving me the echocardiogram, and all of a sudden he stopped and said, "This is the first time I've ever seen a reversal of an enlarged heart."

"You're kidding me," I said, "So I was right! I truly am a different man than I was ten years ago."

The doctor looked me in the eyes and said, "Your heart is as healthy as mine."

So for a guy like me who is already energetic and upbeat, I turned up the notch even higher. Once I left the doctor's office, I added a weight-lifting regimen to my exercise program, and I started memorizing even more challenging content.

I logged on to websites hosted by MIT, Stanford, and Mayo Clinic, and I started learning all I could about the brain. I eventually connected with some of the nation's leading brain experts—people like Robert Ajemian, Ph.D., Research Scientist, McGovern Institute for Brain Research, MIT; James Hardt, Ph.D., Physics and Psychology, Biocybernaut Institute; and Daniel G. Amen, M.D., a double-board-certified psychiatrist, teacher, and nine-time *New York Times* best-selling author.

As my doctor had confirmed—and as I knew inside—I was a transformed man. I owed it all to what would later be called Cogmental Intelligence: a holistic program that improves our mind, body, and emotions.

As I worked toward developing a more powerful mind, I paid close attention to the mind-body-emotions connection, as well. I discovered a way to improve my *entire* body—clearing away stress and stepping up an exercise regimen. A vigorous workout recharged my mind and stimulated the release of endorphins, neurochemicals that actually have an opiatelike effect on our brains. The result: stress relief, clearer thinking, and a healthier body.

＋

Not only did I overcome my "brain cloud"—in other words, my emotional and physical challenges—I ended up growing into what some would call a real-life *Phenomenon*. (Yep, I can't help it— another nineties flick!)

Today, I've logged more than five thousand shows as a mentalist, a magician, and a motivational speaker. I've stood on stages and met so many interesting people—from famous actors and musicians like Tom Hanks and Steven Tyler to sports legends like Shaquille O'Neal. I've achieved dreams that I never thought were possible.

I'm truly humbled that my "better mind, better life" message is resonating with people from all walks of life—everyone from Hollywood actors and pro athletes to Ivy League academics and ordinary folks alike.

Through the years, I've learned that we must treat our *entire* bodies. There's a mind-body-emotions connection that can't be overlooked. As we work toward improving our health, we must exercise both our bodies and our minds.

With three truths under your belt from the last chapter—and after hearing more of my story—here are three challenges I want you to embrace:

Challenge #1: Determine What Steps You Can Take to Improve

If I can do it, you can too!

So here I was with a challenging start on life and so many strikes against me: I wasn't a great student, I struggled in school, I was bullied, and I worked at the steel mill. It was really magic that grew my sense of self. My self-esteem then helped me in business, with Avon.

But, it's not until I got sick when I was forty-nine years old, in 2002, that my brain really started to grow.

Challenge #2: Develop a Plan to Get You Started (and Incentives to Keep You Going)

You'll have plenty of opportunities to do this as you study this book. Don't worry—I'll help you along the way! Customizing a personal plan to improve your mind, body, and emotions begins by setting some goals. (We'll explore this in detail in Chapter 6.)

For now, and as a way of getting you into a goal-setting mind-set, here are five suggestions to get you started. (By the way, each one is approved by my friends at Harvard Medical School.)[15]

1. *Identify what you'd like to change.* For example, the news that my heart was in trouble motivated me to (1) exercise, (2) change my diet, and (3) clear away stress in my life. We're much more likely to succeed if we set priorities that are compelling to us and feel attainable at present.

2. *Choose the first thing you want to change.* For me, it was my sedentary lifestyle. Exercising daily on the stationary bike was my first goal. So here's what I recommend: Select a choice that feels like a sure bet. Like me, do you want to eat healthier? Then adjust your diet. As doctors at Harvard Medical School recommend, it's best to concentrate on just one choice at a time. When a certain change fits into your life comfortably, you can then focus on the next change.

3. *Commit yourself.* Make a written or verbal promise to yourself and one or two supporters you don't want to let down: your partner or child, a teacher, doctor, boss, or friends. That will encourage you to slog through tough spots. Be

explicit about the change you've chosen and why it matters to you. If it's a step toward a bigger goal, include that too. *I'm making a commitment to my health by planning to take a mindful walk, two days a week. This is my first step to a bigger goal: doing a stress-reducing activity every day (and it helps me meet another goal: getting a half hour of exercise every day). I want to do this because I sleep better, my mood improves, and I'm more patient with family and friends when I ease the stress in my life.*

4. *Be proactive and strategize how you can overcome setbacks.* This step alone can help you to be successful. Do some trouble-shooting and plan ways of breaking down possible barriers. For example, not enough time? *I'll get up 20 minutes early for exercises and fit in a 10-minute walk before lunch.* Cupboard bare of healthy choices? *I'll think about five to ten healthy foods I enjoy and will put them on my grocery list.*

5. *Plan a simple reward.* Remember the incentives I provided the kids I spoke to? (Flip back to the opening story in Chapter 2.) Is there a reward you might enjoy for a job well done? For example, if you hit most or all of your marks on planned activities for one week, you'll treat yourself to a splurge with money you saved by quitting smoking, a luxurious bath, or just a double helping of the iTunes application.

Challenge #3: Defeat Negativity

How to Defeat Negativity

- Think about something else that requires concentration!
- Physically destroy your negative thoughts! Write down your negative thoughts on a piece of paper and burn it or throw it away.
- Have a cup of tea.

Embrace the Positive

- Having positive people around you is very important!
- Avoid negative people!
- Do not under estimate the power of positive thought!
- Rewire your brain to be happy by thinking about three things that make you feel grateful. Do this consistently for 21 days in a row.

LET'S TAKE OUR MINDS TO THE NEXT LEVEL

Stress and negativity have serious consequences. Yet we can break free from their grip and take the first few steps toward change. It all begins in our minds. Two of the myths we must bust are that we're not smart enough and that we're too weak. A third myth is equally destructive: It's too late—we're just too old.

4

Myth-Buster: "I'm Too Old"

I'm Stronger, Smarter, and More Alive—In My Sixties!

While I was at an event in Indianapolis, a buddy of mine—a guy named John who lived in the area—called and asked me to join him for a very special lunch. He was giddy, and kept putting an emphasis on the word *special*.

"You can't leave town until you've met a certain lady who is very, very *special*," he said.

"Okay," I replied, wondering what he was up to. "Do my wife and I know her? Is she a celebrity, a relative . . . an Indy car racer?"

"Nope," he said. "But she's a big fan of yours. Her name is Jeanne and she's sixty-nine years old. Just wait 'til you meet her. You're going to be blown away!"

I had no idea what was going on, but I agreed to have lunch with this lady. "Okay then. Tomorrow afternoon it is."

The next day, John and I arrived at Jeanne's house, a simple Midwestern home in the suburbs of the "Racing Capital of the World." As I stepped into her living room, I was greeted by twenty smiling faces—some of her relatives, her husband, and her son. And there was Jeanne with an even bigger grin on her face. She was seated right in the middle of the crowd.

Is this a show? I wondered. *Am I about to do an impromptu magic act?*

Jeanne was excited and full of energy—so I liked her right way. And the second I took a seat right next to her, she tapped my arm and said, "Okay, give me a number from one to fifty."

At first, I didn't know what she was talking about, but I obliged her anyway. "How about two," I said.

Her eyes sparkled and she replied, "Pennsylvania, the capitol is Harrisburg."

Suddenly, it hit me. I instantly knew what she was doing. "You're familiar with my memory program," I said. One of my memory tricks teaches people how to learn the states of the union.

She said, "Give me another number."

"Hmmm . . . how about eleven."

"New York, the capital is Albany," she responded.

Next, I said, "Ten."

Jeanne responded with "Virginia."

Her memory was amazing, and I was completely blown away—just as John said I'd be.

Then she asked for a higher number. I didn't know what she meant by that because I'd only gone up to thirteen at the time. So I said, "Fifty."

She replied, "Hawaii—the capitol is Honolulu."

Jeanne had taken my memory skills program to a higher level, and I couldn't have been more proud of her. I leaned over and gave her a big hug. As I looked around, I sensed that something extraordinary was happening.

Here was what I didn't know: Just six months earlier, she had been in the fight of her life, battling stage four cancer. Learning this ripped my heart in two. I couldn't believe it. Yet my friend John had gotten her interested in my memory program. Along the way, Jeanne had learned all about my story—especially about my own past health problems. She'd discovered how my life was completely transformed as I exercised my mind and my body. So she refused to let a life-threatening illness get the best of her and decided to set off on a similar path.

At first, Jeanne was weakened and discouraged by her illness, yet hearing my story inspired her, and she was instantly drawn to my brain games and memory techniques. She began by taking some gradual steps: short walks around the house, followed by limited memory techniques—whatever her mind and body could handle each day.

Little by little, she took bigger steps and engaged in harder memory challenges. Eventually, Jeanne began to feed more information into her brain—all kinds of interesting facts and figures, including the capitals of all fifty states! She even got her husband and family excited about improving their minds and bodies.

Just days before I had the pleasure of meeting her, doctors gave Jean the greatest news of all: "Your cancer is in remission!"

✦

Jeanne was a miracle!

At age sixty-nine—and in spite of being the victim of a killer disease—she was beating the odds. Jeanne had vitality and energy again . . . and she simply wouldn't stop fighting for her life. This amazing lady inspired me. I can't begin to describe in words what I felt when I heard her story and got to witness her powerful memory. Unfortunately, before this book went to press, Jeanne passed away. With a sharper mind, she enjoyed several years of quality life before her death in May 2018. I am grateful for her drive and spirit—and I will never forget her.

It's no surprise that our brain's ability to form dendrites declines and brain drain sets in as we age. Yet here's what people like Jean and I have discovered: We can take the steps right now to improve our minds and increase our brain power.

Today I'm in my sixties, and I'm stronger, smarter, and more alive!

Jeanne and I are proof that it's never too late and we're never too old to strengthen our bodies and our minds—and nothing is stopping any of us from having a better quality of life. Today, I travel around the world with the USO, helping soldiers with PTSD and brain trauma. In addition, I have achieved so many things that I never thought were attainable for me—that is, until I boosted my brain power.

At this point, you know my story. You know that nearly two decades ago, I gathered the courage to put my factory-working days behind me, and I launched a career as a mentalist, entertaining audiences with mind tricks and my highly developed intuitive abilities. But when I performed for wounded soldiers in a hospital, and was able to catch one man's attention when no one else could, I realized I needed to use my abilities to help wounded minds. And that's my focus today. I speak in a wide range of settings—from corporate retreats and senior care facilities to medical symposiums and the Pentagon—and I teach my brain-boosting systems to everyone from children to neurologists.

I've taken my message and my skills to Massachusetts Institute of Technology where I've worked alongside world-class neurologists. And as a way of demonstrating the power of my memory systems, I even learned Mandarin in six months . . . and then gave a presentation in the language!

Not too bad for a steelworker-turned–memory expert. Not bad at all!

The Hippocampus Connection

As you explore this subject with me, you are going to learn about a very important area of the brain called the hippocampus. Not only does it play an important role in the formation of new memories, but it regulates mood, as well as our spatial awareness. The hippocampus is a small seahorse-shaped organ that's located within the brain's medial temporal lobe and forms an important part of the limbic system, the region that regulates emotions.

So what's the big deal, and why should we care much about this part of our body? Because it affects the kinds of things you are going to learn in this book.

Dr. Daniel Amen and other medical experts generally agree that the hippocampus is involved in declarative memory: memories that can be stated verbally, such as facts and figures. Yet here's something interesting: Their studies have shown that damage to the hippocampus does not affect a person's ability to learn a new skill such as playing a musical instrument or solving certain types of puzzles, which suggests that the memories involved in learning a procedure are governed by brain areas other than the hippocampus.

In the next section, we are going to explore memory exercises that utilize what's known as the anchor system. You see, memory works through association. If we can associate a list of terms or names and faces with certain anchors, then it's more likely to stick.

For example, there's a famous system called the Sun Anchor System. It goes something like this: "One . . . Sun. Two . . . Shoe. Three . . . Tree. Four . . . Door." Anchors like these make it so much easier to remember lists and big chunks of information. (I could add a grocery list to these anchors and come home with exactly what I set out to buy.)

Another famous system is the Roman Room, which is a variation of (but very similar to) a Memory Palace. With this system we can learn to remember lists and associate them with rooms in your house. I use that to remember the twelve best memories of my life. So if I'm having a bad day or I have a bad attitude, and I want to change my state immediately, I just walk through my house (figuratively, of course) and find those twelve best memories. It immediately changes my attitude.

Okay, so there's a good chance that you're staring at this page with a blank expression and thinking, Is this guy crazy? What on earth is he talking about? If so, don't worry. I'll explain this technique (and a few others) in Chapter 6. I'll also tell you about a website and an online memory course that will walk you through them in so much more detail.

When I was first exposed to this system, I had never read a book on anything like this, or studied anybody else's memory techniques. In the early days, as I rode my stationary bike—flip back to Chapter 3 for the full story—my intention wasn't to improve my memory. Instead, I did it in order to keep from becoming bored. I mean, for me, all this memory stuff just happened accidently, yet it clicked . . . and it ultimately transformed my life. And that's what is so amazing about my plan: It's easy to apply to our lives, and it works. But my approach goes way beyond just improving our memory. My plan takes a holistic mind-body-emotions approach that can improve your entire body—and change your life forever.

I must admit, my plan is unique.

It involves a matrix that is so fresh and so new and so unique that I couldn't wait to share it with others—people like Jean (the amazing seventy-year-old you met at the beginning of this chapter).

Following my plan will enable you to memorize all kinds of facts, figures, blocks of information, names, dates, birthdays, addresses—just about anything you need to remember. In other words, it will enable you to sharpen your memory so you can recall the things that you actually care about, and it will help you bust the myths and achieve an overall better quality of life—regardless of your IQ, your health, or your age.

It's time for a quick review, and then it's time to get started!

You've learned some truths in Chapter 2, and you've been given some challenges in Chapter 3. Are you ready to see some results?

If you just nodded yes, here's what you can expect.

Result #1: You Can Become a Better Version of Yourself

It all begins by taking one simple step in a positive new direction. That's what I did when I found myself yearning for adventure and desiring a life filled with meaning and purpose. I couldn't just stuff away those feelings; I had to muster up the courage to do something about them. So I pushed aside that negative voice reminding me that I'm too old, and I took a step toward a new life. It happened during my steel mill days . . .

I met a street magician named Jim Cellini at the Allentown Fair. I was instantly mesmerized by him, and we became good friends. Cellini invited me to Manhattan to bend a 60-penny nail (a hot-galvanized nail that builders use in construction projects). He even challenged me to put my hand in a fox trap during his street performance.

It was an illusion, of course, designed to scare the crowds. In one clean motion, I shoved my hand into it.

SNAP!

The device clamped down on my arm, and I put my acting skills to work—screaming and writhing in pain . . . when, in fact, I wasn't. I admit, it did hurt a little, but not unbearably.

"I need a volunteer to free this man from the trap," Cellini said to the crowd.

With a stranger's help, I struggled a bit to release my hand and then, voilà . . . I was loose with my arm intact, unbloodied, and pain-free.

It was a huge honor to work with the greatest street magician of all time. That experience motivated me to become an entertainer.

I also met the Mighty Atom (Joseph Greenstein) at the Allentown Fair. After watching this eighty-year-old guy bend a 60-penny nail with his bare hands—using nothing but a handkerchief—I knew I had to pursue my dream. It absolutely boggled my mind as I watched him bend the nail so effortlessly. I was on a mission: Learn about the incredible power of the human mind.

Soon I grabbed a box of 60-penny nails from the steel mill and went to work, seeing if I had what it takes to bend them. I tried hundreds of times, failing to put even a small dent in them. In spite of bloodied palms, I had an intense desire and passion. I never gave up!

One day, out of nowhere, the spike bent like butter in my hands. This accomplishment alone set me on my new path. I had discovered that nothing is impossible. We can accomplish anything with a positive mind-set and a never-give-up attitude.

Between the Mighty Atom and Cellini, I combined both men's acts into one unique show and began my career as the Madman of Magic and the Psychic Madman. Today, I'm still bending the 60-penny nails and hope to continue doing so well into my seventies—just like the one and only Mighty Atom. What an inspiration both men have been in my life and my career.

Result #2: You Can Learn *How* to Learn

It's important to understand that we all learn in different ways. Some of us absorb information quickly, while others need a little more time to ponder, reflect, and explore. Neither style is better than the other; we're all different and different is good!

So the first step toward learning something new is to be self-aware of our learning styles and preferences. Once I accept what makes me uniquely me, as well as my approach to grasping something unfamiliar, I can get on with the process of *learning*!

Next, it's important to utilize memory techniques such as one called *chunking.* (More on this in Chapter 6 and the Appendix of this book.) This memory technique offers a great method for memorizing long strings of information by breaking it down into compact packages our mind can easily access. For most people, short-term memory can't handle more than seven to nine items at a time. So with this method, chunks build on chunks, nurturing learning and knowledge.

Lastly, we need to let go of stress. Negativity can get us stuck in a mental rut, filling us with self-doubt and anxiety, both of which are toxic for learning. Anxiety blocks thinking and stalls us from learning and making new connections. Our knowledge will soar if we keep and stay positive. We would be wise to view learning as exploration. It will give us a sense of determination, which we can turn into grit when the going gets tough.

Result #3: You Can Turn Back the Clock

The fountain of youth exists, and the path to it is found by engaging in mind-body exercises. As I said earlier, I discovered this powerful duo more than a decade ago while doing brain games on my stationary bike. As we employ mind-body exercises, we will become healthier, our confidence will soar, and our thinking will become much sharper.

Physical exercise has so many benefits: It restores youthful metabolism, lowers stress, induces feel-good hormones, rejuvenates the heart and strengthens our bones. Likewise, challenging our minds with brain games and exercises can sharpen our thinking and keep us mentally fit. This book is all about helping you to achieve these goals.

LET'S TAKE OUR MINDS TO THE NEXT LEVEL

Now that you have heard my story and followed my path to a better mind, we're ready to customize a brain-boosting plan that can work for you.

TRANSFORMATION STARTS NOW

A Conversation with Daniel Amen, M.D.

Dr. Amen is both a friend and a supporter of my memory program. He invited me to share my story and memory skills on "Jim Karol's Memory Master Course"—a seven-lesson online series. This highly interactive course (http://memorymastercourse.com) brings the pages of this book to life. It harnessess the power of building memory reserves to reap the lifelong benefits of neuroplasticity—the brain's ability to form new connections and brain cells when learning something new.

Dr. Amen and I share the same passion: helping people of all ages improve their minds and ultimately their lives. What we want to teach you in these pages (and in my online course) is how you can improve and expand your memory—and ultimately strengthen your brain.

Here are highlights of a conversation we shared during my course:

Jim Karol: What I'm about to teach you will actually give you an edge on everybody at work or at school. Actually, it doesn't matter if you're a student or if you just want to stay mentally sharp. It doesn't matter if you're five or ninety-five; these skills will help develop your brain health.

Daniel Amen: We are going to help see how your lifestyle impacts your brain health. Including the right diet, exercise, and sleep. But this is so much more. This is the single best thing you can do to harness the power of your brain's ability to get strong by learning. It actually enhances something called neuroplasticity. So if you're learning a new skill, we'll teach you plenty. If you enjoy playing brain games, we'll teach you how to get the most out of them. Learning all of this can make a dramatic difference in your confidence, in your self-esteem, and in your ability to learn new information.

Jim: It's going to be easy to do, and it will increase your focus. What I reveal will increase your energy, your memory.

Daniel: This course is based on time-tested results, the latest scientific evidence that can help you to strengthen your memory and create synaptic connections. These are the connections between brain cells. What we teach will help your brain to grow new neurons. We are going to talk a lot about the hippocampus—the horseshoe-shaped structure on the inside of our temporal lobes. The hippocampus helps get memory into long-term storage. It's one of the only parts of the brain that actually grows new neurons every day.

Jim: It will change your life forever. Trust me. It changed my life. I don't know where I'd be today if it weren't for this stuff.

Daniel: There are so many things you can benefit from. If you're a student, if you're at work somewhere, if you're older and want to keep your memory sharp. This is a course that can help you keep your brain sharp. And it's drop-dead fun. The benefits are to increase your focus and energy and to sharpen and enhance your memory. It's all designed to make it stronger.

Jim: This will increase your creativity. And my favorite, it will increase your intuition.

Daniel: Also, it enables you to think faster. We have exercises to improve processing speed. You will obviously gain more knowledge.

Jim: And for me, it built my confidence. This was definitely the biggest confidence-builder I had. As you know, I was shy and backward. What we discuss here built up my confidence. What's more, you can impress your friends with this, and wow, there is so much you can do with this. And it's incredible. It changed my life.

Daniel: And another benefit is—as you work your memory center in your brain (again, it's called the hippocampus)—you will experience improved moods and a greater sense of well-being. We can teach you an exercise that can change your mood almost immediately. I love that. One thing that you told me is that when your memory is better, your aim is better. So if you're playing golf, throwing darts, if you're playing pool, shooting baskets, you can improve your athletic skills when you have a better brain. You have a better memory, but everything else in your life is better as well.

> "Jim has done some really special and amazing things; he's a big guy with a big heart, which—today—has nothing to do with cardiomyopathy! What he has to teach you will blow your mind. When I first met him, my head was spinning, but I was so excited to be able to share his plan with my audience and the people I serve and care about."
>
> —Daniel Amen, M.D.

Part Two

+

MY MEMORY
MAGIC PLAN

5

Welcome to the World of Cogmental Intelligence

Combining the Best of Emotional Intelligence with the Study of Mentalism, Memory, Cognition, and Deception Detection

Tyler flipped open a notebook, instinctively clicked his pen a couple of times, and then looked up at the ten coworkers gathered around a long conference room table. He leaned forward and began to speak. "Thanks for joining me this morning," he said, studying each face staring back at him. "I know you're all busy, so I'll get right to the point. Our CEO asked me to put together an unstoppable, best-of-the-best, superhuman sales team that's going to help me take over the world!"

Nervous laughter rose from the table. Tyler grinned big.

"Well," the fiftysomething VP continued, "maybe not the whole world—but definitely the tech world. Four of you are going to join me in London next month for the meeting of a lifetime. We're going to win over one of the financial world's leading investment companies and turn our tiny technology firm into a major player."

A few eyes grew wide, while a couple squinted. All around the table, Tyler spotted fidgeting hands, furrowed foreheads, shifting bodies, lip-licking, deep sighs—right along with some confidence cues that caught his attention: flashbulb eyes with genuine smiles, shoulders leaning forward, and steepling hands (fingertip to fingertip).

Tyler quickly jotted some names on the right side of his notebook: *Sherri, Jenny, David, and Alec—most likely YES!* On the left side he wrote, *Dan, Steve, Scott, Christie, Staci, and Nicole—most likely NO!*

"So I'm going to chat privately with each one of you to gauge your interest in joining my little team," he said. "I have to work fast and select four of you right away. Are you with me? Are you all up for what I promise will be a painless interview?"

"Absolutely!" a couple of folks shouted back. Others nodded and gave thumbs-up signs.

By the end of the workday, Tyler's instincts proved *mostly* right. After spending five to ten minutes with each person, Tyler scratched out David's name, replacing him with Scott, and switched out Jenny with Christie.

At first glance, David seemed to have everything the VP was looking for: confidence, a professional appearance, and the impression that he could close the deal. But within seconds of interacting with him, Tyler knew the young salesman wouldn't be a good fit.

The first clue was his body language. It screamed "immaturity, disrespect . . . arrogance." When David stepped into Tyler's office and took a seat, he didn't sit up and politely look his superior in the eye. Instead, he began to splay out in the chair with his head turned toward the window. (This is often interpreted as a territorial display.)

"So this is the view from the big corner office," David said with a smirk and just a hint of sarcasm in his voice. The young man finally sat up and leaned forward. "Yeah . . . I could get used to this," he said, flashing a smile. Yet his mouth seemed closed and tight, and the rest of his face didn't light up.

"In all honesty," he continued, "I'm your man. I'll work hard, and I'll win the client."

At this point, sirens were going off in Tyler's head, and his "internal deception detector" was on full alert. David's words simply didn't match his demeanor and tone, and his attitude underscored the young man's indifference to those in authority.

Suddenly, remembering that David had a reputation for being cocky, Tyler flipped open an HR file on him. Yet as he scanned through it, he was blown away that everything seemed to check out on paper. Even David's sales quotas were good.

Still, Tyler refused to be duped or falsely won over. His intuition and emotional intelligence had kicked in and he knew what had to be done. Tyler swallowed hard, shut the folder, and then underlined the word NO on his notepad.

"Thanks for your willingness to meet with me," he said. "I've made my decision, and you won't be on my team."

A short time later, Christie popped into Tyler's office. During the morning gathering, she sat at the table hunched over, appearing weak and insecure. Her shoulders rose toward her ears, causing a "turtle effect." Her eyes were downcast, and she constantly rubbed her forehead.

But the woman who was now standing in his office seemed just the opposite.

Christie was confident, engaging, and witty—not weak at all. She smiled and looked Tyler in the eye, convincing him that she'd be a perfect addition to the team. So what caused the dramatic turn-around? Moments before attending the earlier meeting, Christie had learned that a close friend was being tested for a terminal illness. Later, she received word that her friend's medical condition was curable. The emotional trauma was over, and Christie was relieved. She was back to being herself again.

During Tyler's brief interview with her, he was able to understand the context of her emotions and decode her behavior. Tyler applied the same observational effort to Christie as he had with David . . . and was able to accurately speed-read his coworker.

By the end of the day, Tyler had found the best-of-the-best and was free to engage his superhuman sales team. Next up: Take over the tech world!

Ultimate Memory, Ultimate Results

Imagine walking into a room full of total strangers and quickly cluing in to key details about their lives—almost as if you could read their minds! Imagine looking into someone's eyes and being able to detect if they are lying or telling the truth. Best of all, imagine your brain growing stronger and more powerful every day, enabling you to sharpen your thinking and regain your mental edge . . . and even accomplish tasks both physically and mentally that you once thought impossible. This is what my Memory Magic plan delivers, and it's exactly what men and women like Tyler have discovered. So what's making the difference?

Four brain-boosting steps that have enabled them to:

1. *Enhance Memory*—acquire more knowledge, sharpen their thinking, and then clearly reproduce and recall what they've learned.

2. *Rev Up Energy*—incorporate vigorous workouts into their lives that recharge their minds and stimulate the release of neurochemicals that relieve stress and promote clearer thinking.

3. *Build Better Relationships*—connect with and relate to people on a deeper level through reading body language and detecting deception . . . as well as identifying their own and other people's emotions, understanding them, and being able to manage them.

4. *Increase Intuition*—clear away stress and engage in creative thinking.

Cogmental Intelligence will not only help you to improve memory and cognition, it will enable you to read people and improve relationships. But as we work toward developing a more powerful mind, we'll pay close attention to the mind-body-emotions connection, as well. My program focuses on improving our *entire* body—helping you manage stress and improve your physical well-being. A vigorous workout recharges our minds and stimulates the release of endorphins, neurochemicals that actually have an opiatelike effect on our brains. The result: stress relief and clearer thinking.

Using Tyler as a case study, let's move in for a closer look at how my plan can radically shape each one of us into healthier, happier, much more energetic individuals.

ACHIEVING THE MENTAL EDGE

Tyler didn't always have a sharp mind. It seemed as if the older he got, the more he began to forget things—people, places, even special moments in his life. Celebrating his fiftieth birthday was yet another reminder that his memory was fading.

"Quick—what were we doing on this very night . . . ten years ago?" his wife asked as they crawled into bed. It was late, and the couple had just said good-bye to their last dinner guest.

"I can't remember what we did ten minutes ago," Tyler said. "I need a hint."

"We were on the island of Antigua, taking a long walk on the beach," his wife explained. "We ended up all alone . . . in a hidden cove."

"Hmmm—I remember visiting lots of beaches on an island that has 365 of them," Tyler said. Then he raised his eyebrows. "But a hidden cove? Tell me more!"

His wife sat up. "You seriously don't remember?"

Tyler shrugged his shoulders.

"Shame on you," she said with wink and a half smile. "It was your fortieth birthday, and we'd just celebrated with a perfect meal and that gorgeous sunset—"

"At the beachside restaurant," Tyler interrupted. "I'm starting to remember now. Go on."

"We grabbed a bottle of zinfandel and two glasses and went for a long walk by the Caribbean Sea. We found ourselves in a cove."

This time Tyler sat up. "The full moon lit up the white sand," he said. "We shared some wine and watched the cruise ships on the horizon."

"And we talked half the night about our dreams," his wife added. "That's when you decided to do something about all the stress you were under at work and make a career change. That's when you took the steps to make us a stronger family."

Tyler slumped back on his pillow, feeling a mix of joy . . . and bewilderment. The memory that his wife had shared was the perfect gift, yet he couldn't help worrying that his mind was starting to slip. Anxious thoughts began to swirl through his brain . . .

How is it that an experience she had cherished and remembered as if it were yesterday is now just a faded collection of snapshots tucked away in the back of my brain?

And what's with the constant brain freeze?

Why do I struggle to remember so many things—names, faces . . . important moments?

Tyler had taken steps a decade ago to reduce stress and to put his family first. Now, he was determined to improve his mind and his body.

✦

Your memories shape you. Who you are and how it feels to be uniquely you—all your hopes, dreams, fears, and quirks alike—are strengthened by your memories. "Like a character made of Legos, we're built of blocks of memory that all fit together to form our consciousness," explains Chris Heath, M.D., a psychiatrist and psychoanalyst in Dallas, Texas. "How can it be otherwise? How can we say hello to someone or lean in to kiss someone new without evoking memories of previous greetings and kisses?"[16]

So it isn't surprising that Tyler, and countless others like him, feel so frustrated by constant brain freeze. The fact is, memory loss is a loss of self, and it's why concerns about declining thinking and memory skills rank among the top fears people have as they age.[17]

How about you?

Like Tyler, maybe you feel as if you're losing your identity as special memories slip away year after year. Maybe you're tired of misplacing items and wasting precious time hunting for them. Maybe you're sick of the embarrassment that comes with forgetting someone's name or the details of their lives. The good news is, our minds can improve and even grow stronger. I'm proof of that. Scientifically speaking, the silver bullet that has transformed my life, as well as the lives of men and women of all ages and walks of life, is simple, yet powerful: a daily cognitive fitness regimen.

According to researchers at Harvard Medical School, our genes play a role in brain health, but so do our choices. Proven ways to protect memory and strengthen our minds include following a healthy diet, exercising regularly, and living a mentally active life.[18] That's where my plan can make the biggest difference of all. Just as muscles grow stronger with use, a program of cognitive fitness—exercising our brains daily—helps keep mental skills and memory toned up.

In this section, we'll move in for a closer look, and I'll show you how to customize brain workouts that will have the greatest impact; activities that require you to stop being a mental couch potato—in other words, cut back on passive activities like watching TV—so you can stimulate those neurons and achieve a more youthful functioning brain. You'll choose from an arsenal of intellectual challenges that will fit your interests and personality.

Here are the brain-boosting steps we'll cover in Chapter 6:

Acquiring Knowledge. You'll feel as if you're back in grade school as you fill your head with interesting facts and figures and practical information—everything from learning the capitals of American states to strengthening your vocabulary to memorizing poems or passages from the Bible.

Learning New Skills. Ever desire to pick up a new language or learn how to grow a vegetable garden or master the basic steps of ballroom dancing? Now is the time to stop thinking about these activities and to start pursuing them—for your brain's sake. (I'll help you work up a plan.) It's essential that we use our brains by challenging ourselves mentally. Learning a new skill does just that.

Engaging the Senses. Incorporating all five of our senses into memory techniques can stimulate the brain and improve our ability to recall information. The most powerful senses for recall are sight, sound, and smell. We'll explore how engaging our senses can sharpen our thinking and beef up problem-solving.

Becoming More Social. The happiest people are those who connect daily with friends and family. They are also the smartest. Why? Interpersonal communication engages our emotions and stimulates our brains because we are social creatures; our brains are wired that way. And as author Henry Cloud, Ph.D., points out, relationships are our most fundamental need, the very foundation of who we are. Without it, he says, "We can't be truly human."[19] As a precursor to a more detailed look at improving relationships (see "Building Better Relationships" below, as well as Chapter 9), we'll look at simple, practical ways of becoming more social—and why this step invigorates the brain.

Incorporating Brain Exercises. The options are seemingly endless in today's marketplace, but I'll equip you with the best of the best—dozens of games, puzzles, mental exercises, and little-known tricks that will improve your cognitive fitness.

RESTORING YOUTHFUL METABOLISM

With a spotter at his side, Tyler gripped the barbell and pushed with every ounce of strength within him. It was 6:00 a.m., and he was working out before heading to the office. He and his best friend had been hitting the weights three mornings a week for the past several months, and his commitment was finally paying off. But when he first started, he was met with plenty of skeptics—mostly from other fiftysomething guys at work.

"Sounds like midlife crisis all over again," his boss jabbed. "Don't break a hip keeping up with the kids."

His older assistant handed him a protein-replacement drink. "Take this," he said. "You're gonna need it more than me!"

Instead of getting upset, Tyler used their jabs as a motivation to prove them wrong. *Too old, too weak*, he fumed, as he attacked the bench press. *They're going to eat their words.*

For six months now, he'd been taking out his frustration on the weights. (That, too, was paying off.) Today he was benching 115 pounds and had reached his fourteenth rep.

"Come on, Tyler, go for it," his friend said to him. "One more and you've hit a new record."

"AAARRRGGG!" he groaned as he eked out the final rep.

"That's a new record!" his friend shouted. "You did it! You've lifted the most weight yet ... along with the most repetitions! You're growing stronger"

No doubt about it, Tyler had been pushing himself. And whenever he looked in a mirror, he could see the difference too. His body was becoming leaner and his muscles were getting firmer. Mostly, he had more energy, and he felt better. His mind was growing stronger too.

"Well done," a twentysomething onlooker told him, slapping him on the back.

Tyler decided right then and there that he wouldn't be defined by negative labels. Instead, he'd make every effort to be the healthiest, most youthful, best person he could be regardless of his age. He also decided that he'd continue being exactly who he should be—*himself*!

✦

It's no secret that our hearts and muscles benefit from regular exercise, but medical evidence keeps mounting that working out is good for our brains too. Aerobic exercise appears to improve a person's cognitive function, and resistance training can enhance a person's executive function and memory.

"There is now a wide body of research showing that the benefits to the body with exercise also exist for the brain," says study author Joe Northey, a Ph.D. candidate at the University of Canberra Research Institute for Sport and Exercise in Australia. "When older adults undertake aerobic or resistance exercise, we see changes to the structure and function of areas of the brain responsible for complex mental tasks and memory function."[20]

Our bodies are designed to be active, so I've made exercise a key part of my Memory Magic Plan. From stretching, stress release, and Memitation (more on this later) to vigorous workouts, I'll show you that the harder we work our bodies and the better the nutrients we put into them, the leaner, stronger, and more energetic they will become—regardless of our age. And our minds benefit too. More blood flows to our brains, which helps to create new brain cells. The protein BDNF (brain-derived neurotrophic factor) also seems to play a role because it helps repair and protect brain cells from degeneration. And exercise boosts our mood by triggering the release of feel-good hormones and chemicals, like endorphins, that can improve our brain health.[21]

Here are the brain-boosting steps we'll cover in Chapter 7:

Launching Aerobic Activity. The technical definition is "training with oxygen." In other words, an activity that gets your heart pumping and air flowing through your body: walking, hiking, jogging, swimming, bicycling, or cross-country skiing. The benefits are indisputable: (1) stronger hearts, (2) lower blood pressure, (3) improved metabolism, (4) burned-off fat stores, and (5) a rush of endorphins.

Launching Anaerobic Exercise. This means "training without oxygen," and it involves all forms of high-intensity activity that are engaged in for short periods of time. Examples include sprinting, resistance training (working out with weights), powerlifting, tennis, racquetball . . . and any other sport you can think of that causes fatigue to the muscles with harder but shorter bursts of energy. During anaerobic exercise, our cardiovascular system has a challenging time delivering the necessary levels of oxygen to our muscles fast enough. And since muscles require air to maintain prolonged exertion, anaerobic exercises can only continue for short periods of time. Why is it important for overall good health? Resistance training, for example, provides these benefits: (1) muscle strength, (2) a lean, toned body, (3) weight loss, and (4) stress reduction.

Fueling a Healthier Mind. A well-balanced diet is crucial to good health, and it will enable you to fuel your body—which, in turn, will lead to stronger brain function. Certain foods and drinks can stimulate cognitive function. For example, diets rich in fish, whole grains, green leafy vegetables, olives, and nuts actually help maintain brain health. We'll explore a variety of brain-boosting super-foods.

Getting More Rest and Sleep. Sleep is absolutely vital to your health and well-being, yet way too many of us are sleep deprived and neglect getting the rest we need. During sleep, you actually recharge your mind and body. It allows your body to recuperate and restore itself from exhaustion. In addition, sleep enables our cells to regenerate and rejuvenate because that's when our bodies secrete growth hormones that repair tissues and organs.

BUILDING BETTER RELATIONSHIPS

A hurried, hassled home life. Overextended schedules. Fast-track living. That's how Tyler once described his life—that is, *before* he set out to make a change.

"I want what we had in Antigua," he told his wife, after returning home from a magical vacation on an island paradise. "We actually slowed down and learned how to savor what we saw. Why can't we do that here?"

His wife nodded her head in agreement. "I'm ready," she said. "And what I want most is what we shared. We connected better and started reading each other. I like what I read!"

Tyler smiled. "It's like our eyes were opened."

Back in the busy world of work and endless meetings, Tyler and his wife felt as if they spent every waking moment in the rat race—running in circles, but not getting anywhere; encountering each other, but not going very deep. They'd spend a typical day racing from appointment to appointment, flying past clients and colleagues, but never really connecting. At home, they ended up neglecting the ones they loved, putting the rat race before family.

The result? Conflict, strained relationships, misunderstandings . . . missed opportunities.

"Our eyes have been opened," Tyler told his wife. "Let's start seeing again."

◆

As Tyler discovered, it's amazing what you can see when you slow down and take the time to observe the world around you—especially the people in your life. You can develop mindfulness, reduce conflict, and improve relationships with friends, family, and coworkers alike.

Open your eyes and you'll see the nonverbal "tells" that can unlock meaningful connections and deepen your empathy for others. In the workplace, careful observation and managing emotions can enable you to stay calm and perform creatively and effectively under pressure—and these skills can ultimately give you the relational edge. What kinds of things will you observe? The movement of a person's hand or foot, excessive blinking, pursing lips, slumped shoulders. Big deal, right? Yes, these emotional clues are a very big deal. Right in front of us are all kinds of important details; subtle tells that could reveal a person's true thoughts and intentions.

Accurately reading people—in other words, cluing in to their nonverbal behaviors in order to assess their thoughts, feelings, and motives—is the part of my Memory Magic Plan that will engage that powerful mind of yours. It takes practice and proper training to master, yet I'm convinced that these are skills that anyone *can* and *should* learn. In fact, researchers and experts claim that those who can effectively read and interpret nonverbal communication, and manage how others perceive them, will enjoy greater success in life than those who lack this skill.[22]

Joe Navarro is one of those experts. He's an ex–FBI agent who spent his entire career decoding nonverbal communication, and he even wrote a best-selling book on the subject: *What Every Body Is Saying*. Amazingly, Joe began deciphering body language when he was just eight years old—not out of fascination, but out of the need to survive. He and his family came to America as exiles from Cuba and were unable to speak English at first. So he did what thousands of other immigrants have done: Joe relied on another language ... nonverbal behavior. He saw the human body as a kind of billboard that transmitted what a person was thinking through gestures, facial expressions, and physical movements that he could read. Here's how Joe describes this revelation in his own words:

> I learned to use body language to decipher what my classmates and teachers were trying to communicate to me and how they felt about me. One of the first things I noticed was that students or teachers who genuinely liked me would raise (or arch) their eyebrows when they first saw me walk into the room. On the other hand, those individuals who weren't too friendly toward me would squint their eyes slightly when I appeared—a behavior that once observed is never forgotten. I used this nonverbal information, as so many other immigrants have, quickly to evaluate and develop friendships, to communicate despite the obvious language barrier, to avoid enemies, and in nurturing healthy relationships. Many years later I would use these same nonverbal eye behaviors to solve crimes as a special agent at the Federal Bureau of Investigation (FBI).[23]

Here are the brain-boosting steps we'll cover in Chapter 8: *Reading Body Language*. One of the keys to achieving that mental edge is socialization. As we discussed earlier, nothing is better for our minds (and our memories) than strong social relationships. And as we just learned, nothing is better for improving relationships than learning how to read people. We'll learn how to speed-read people, and we'll explore the basics of body language: what hands, feet, lips, eyelids, shoulders, and torsos reveal about moods and motives.

Getting to the Truth. Deception detection is a fascinating study of body language that seeks to uncover reliable behavioral indicators of deception—and it, too, is a big part of my program. Those who master this skill end up possessing a powerful key to unlocking truth. Basically, it involves the examination of behaviors such as posture shifts, gaze aversion, and foot and hand movements. With this ability, we can learn how to read others and unlock what they are thinking and feeling.

Pinpointing Emotions. Having the ability to identify and manage the emotional state in others, as well as the ability to effectively manage and control our own thoughts, can improve our interpersonal relationships. And that's what we will explore in Chapter 9. I have combined these abilities with the skills I've learned as a mentalist, not to mention key aspects of deception detection.

SUPERCHARGING INTUITION

Taking the time to stretch and relax—that was Tyler's favorite part of the day.

Most evenings before turning in for the night, he and his wife spent twenty minutes winding down, clearing away stress, and engaging in simple activities that helped relax their minds and their bodies. (Each session varied a bit; some were shorter, while others focused on different relaxation techniques.)

Tyler took a sip of calming peppermint tea. "I looked forward to this all day."

His wife pointed to a bottle of massage oil. "I'm looking forward to what happens later."

"You mean sleep?!" Tyler said with a wink.

Sitting face-to-face on the floor, the couple began with a variety of stretching routines: relaxing stretches for their backs; stretches for their legs, feet, and ankles; as well as stretches for their shoulders and arms. As they spent time stretching, they'd tie in deep breathing with each maneuver. Next, they'd move on to memitation techniques.

Tyler took a breath of air, deep from his gut, and then he let it out. He did this a few times with his eyes closed, slowly breathing in and out . . . concentrating on the air flowing in and out of his lungs. (Tyler continued doing this for about three minutes.) Then he began to focus on a positive thought—something from the day that made him happy. Soon after, he began to review a past experience that he'd committed to memory (another positive thought, of course). As he slowly inhaled and exhaled, he allowed his mind to walk through every detail of that memory—the sights, sounds, smells, and emotions.

Meanwhile, Tyler's wife meditated on Psalm 19:1–2 from the Old Testament, a couple of verses she had memorized; verses that gave her hope: "The heavens keep telling the wonders of God, and the skies declare what he has done. Each day informs the following day; each night announces to the next. . . ."[24] She repeated the verses, pondering each word, and allowing herself to relax with each breath she took.

Gradually, as the couple continued to memitate, they made every effort to clear away toxic stress and to set their minds on calming thoughts. Without even realizing it, their minds and bodies were becoming toned and balanced, ready to heal from a solid night's sleep. What's more, they were supercharging their intuition.

◆

Opening the door to creativity and intuition—and ultimately to a better-working mind—begins as we clear away stress and negativity. As Tyler and his wife demonstrated, the best way to promote relaxation is through a combination of stretching, deep breathing, and Memitation.

Here are the brain-boosting steps we'll cover in Chapter 10:

Clearing Away Stress and Negativity. Deadlines at work and pressures at home produce stress. When this happens, an adrenaline rush surges through our bodies. Our breathing and heart rate jump, our senses become heightened, and we receive an instant burst of energy. But if we remain in this supercharged state for too long, we crash, and we end up feeling all kinds of opposite (and highly unwanted) emotions: vulnerability, uncertainty, insecurity, doubt, fear, worry, stress. The solution: Come down from the hills of stress and into the valleys of rest on a daily basis. Our minds and bodies are not designed for a continual state of fear, worry, and anxiety, but for continual tranquility with short bursts of adrenaline.

Employing Stretching, Deep Breathing, and Memitation Techniques. "It [stretching] is peaceful, relaxing, and noncompetitive," writes fitness expert Bob Anderson in his popular book *Stretching: 30th Anniversary Edition.*[25] "The subtle, invigorating feelings of stretching allow you to get in touch with your muscles. . . . It relaxes your mind and tunes up your body, and it should be part of your daily life." Likewise, breathing properly is essential. We can live for weeks without food, days without water, and how long without air? Maybe six minutes. Air is the very essence of life,[26] and deep breathing is the way we send oxygen into every single cell in our bodies. The result: more energy and sharper thinking. Mix it all up with Memitation, and we have a powerful brain-booster.

Thinking Creatively, Unlocking Intuition. Creative thinking and intuitive inspiration has helped successful people in all walks of life to dream, innovate, and make their mark on the world. You can too. Throughout history, inventors and artists have developed techniques that have enabled them to call upon their genius minds so they could create completely new ideas and turn them into reality. We'll explore some of their secrets.

LET'S TAKE OUR MINDS TO THE NEXT LEVEL

My Memory Magic Plan has been used to help business leaders, professional athletes, law enforcement, and military veterans alike. From enhancing memory and focus to boosting intuition and self-esteem, my program has gained the support of memory experts. Take a look at this: "I wanted to reiterate how profoundly your presentation impacted the neuroscience community here at MIT, particularly the faculty members who study memory! Indeed, in historical terms, you may possess one of the greatest long-term memories ever documented." (Robert Ajemian, Ph.D., Research Scientist, McGovern Institute for Brain Research, MIT)

Are you ready to get started?

With definitions and an overview in mind, let's move into a detailed memory-boosting system that you can personalize and apply to your own life.

MY MEMORY MAGIC PLAN: AT-A-GLANCE STEPS

Brain-Booster No. 1:
Enhance Memory and Sharpen Focus
- Incorporate Brain Exercises
- Acquire Knowledge
- Learn New Skills
- Engage the Senses
- Become More Social

Brain-Booster No. 2:
Rev Up Energy and Self-Esteem
- Launch Aerobic Activity
- Launch Anaerobic Exercise
- Fuel a Healthier Mind

Brain-Booster No. 3:
Pinpoint Hidden Motives
- Read Body Language
- Get to the Truth

Brain-Booster No. 4:
Build Better Relationships
- Exercise Emotional Intelligence: *Consider, Care, Communicate*
- Tune In Verbal and Nonverbal Signals: *Read Body Language, Recognize the Unspoken Subtext of a Conversation, and Nurture the Ability to See and Hear Emotion*
- Identify and Manage Five Basic Emotions: *Happiness, Sadness, Anger, Fear, and Shame*

Brain-Booster No. 5:
Increase Creativity and Intuition
- Clear Away Stress and Negativity
- Employ Stretching, Deep Breathing, and Memitation Techniques
- Think Creatively, Unlock Intuition

6

Brain-Booster No. 1: Enhance Memory and Sharpen Focus

Exploring Brain Games that Exercise
Your Gray Matter

With college behind her now, Amy couldn't wait to begin her first real job: She had accepted a position as a middle-school English teacher in Chicago. The inner-city campus was rough around the edges and was filled with teens who looked more like inmates than students—just the kind of place Amy wanted to be: a school where she thought she could do some good.

"Welcome to Hell!" the principal said with a quick handshake. "Come on. I'll escort you to your classroom. Trust me, you'll need it."

It wasn't the pep talk she thought she'd hear on her first day, and yet it happened. Amy just shrugged off the negativity and walked a bit faster to keep up with the gruff administrator. Even though she had a lot to learn—and lots of details to remember—the twenty-three-year-old was excited to be there.

"Did you know that I grew up near the school?" she told the

principal, as they weaved through a crowded hallway. "I really feel a connection here. In a sense, these are my kids."

Her new boss stopped in his tracks, lowered his glasses, and stared at Amy in disbelief. "Are you saying you were once a student here?"

"Uh, no," Amy said. "My parents sent me to a private school."

The principal winced. "Of course they did."

"But I lived near families whose kids attend here," she added. "I know what these students face every day. I really think I'm going to help make life better for them."

The principal adjusted his glasses and continued walking. "Look," he said, "I appreciate your enthusiasm, but I need you to focus on teaching seventh-grade reading and writing, not changing the world. And try to stick around for more than a month. These kids have already managed to run off two English teachers before you—and we're only halfway through the school year."

When they reached the classroom, the principal flung open the door. Amy wasn't prepared for what she saw. The small room was packed with forty energetic middle-schoolers. Most were Hispanic and Latino immigrants who barely spoke English.

"QUIET!" the principal yelled as he and Amy stepped in front of a murky, whitish-green chalkboard. "And sit down! This is your new teacher, Miss Amy. When I point to you, I want you to tell her your name."

The principal started motioning to each student, and one by one they called out their names: "Ricardo De La Cruz Castro" . . . "Mateo Hernandez Castro" . . . "Lucas Garcia" . . . "Sofia Valentina Lopez" . . . "Isabella Gonzalez" . . .

Amy smiled at each teen. She was genuinely happy to be their teacher—but the classroom was another matter! It was worse than she had imagined, and it was nothing like her childhood schools.

The ceiling was stained with water leaks, and it sagged in places; the paint was peeling off the stark walls, and the air was damp and musty. It wasn't the kind of place that invited learning.

Yet the biggest thing that caught Amy's eye was the number of students packed into the tiny space. *How am I ever going to teach so many kids—for five periods a day?* she wondered. *I'll have to learn Spanish fast because I can't teach if I can't connect. Is that even possible?*

And how will I remember all their names . . . let alone their faces?

The excitement Amy felt when she first set foot on campus was quickly being swallowed up by the countless challenges ahead, and the principal wasn't helping. He leaned over and whispered in her ear: "Like I said: Welcome to—" He silently mouthed the final word.

A worried look washed over her face.

◆

Imagine being in this young teacher's shoes. Before she can settle in and become competent at her new job, she'll need to quickly learn how to navigate a stressful environment, endure negativity from her boss, break through communication barriers . . . *and* memorize a couple hundred names, plus key details of each person's life.

While I can't help her change issues like unreasonable class sizes or improve substandard working conditions, I can help Amy become the best person she can be. I can show her—and *you*—how to sharpen thinking, improve memory, and regain the mental edge needed to thrive under pressure. Boosting our memory enables us to manage people and to solve problems.

One of the most frequently asked questions I receive is, "How can I learn to remember names and faces?" Not remembering someone's name, as well as the details of another person's life, is not only embarrassing, it can hinder meaningful connections with others.

It's an essential skill for teachers like Amy—and anyone in a people profession.

Here's another question people ask me: "How can I stop losing things—like my cell phone and car keys—and stop forgetting appointments?"

Improving our memory can really help us to prevent these annoying situations. Just as physical exercise is important for our bodies, mental exercise is extremely important for a healthy brain, and my students see results after just a few weeks of exercising their minds.

In the remainder of this chapter, I'll guide you through some of the most effective brain-boosters. Here's what I include in the mix: (1) a weekly brain exercise that involves a game or a puzzle—something that challenges our thinking and requires us to solve a problem, (2) techniques that keep our brain cells on their toes as we memorize facts and acquire new information, (3) focus training, and (4) exercises designed to increase creativity, knowledge, and intuition.

Let's begin with a quiz. Don't worry—it's one that I guarantee you'll pass! (But I can't promise that you'll like the results.) The goal is to help you assess your own brain function, and to think deeply about your own mind. Is it active or on autopilot? Are you absorbing new information every day? Are you challenging your brain?

The quiz below will help you to assess where you are now—and where you want to be in three months. You'll gain a snapshot of not only how often you forget things, but also to what extent it's affecting your life. If much of your life is severely impacted by forgetfulness and a cloudy mind, it's a good idea to get a thorough exam from your family doctor before you get started.

Please read each question and think about how often each statement has been true of you in the past month.

MEMORY SELF-ASSESSMENT

	Never	Sometimes	Often	Always
I am always forgetting appointments, dates, and details of projects I'm working on.	0	1	2	3
No matter how hard I try, I constantly forget names and faces of acquaintances, clients, and coworkers.	0	1	2	3
I forget things all the time.	0	1	2	3
Even when I remind myself to remember something, I still end up forgetting it.	0	1	2	3
Brain freeze frustrates me.	0	1	2	3
I am always stressed and preoccupied about something.	0	1	2	3
Negative thoughts bombard my mind.	0	1	2	3
I avoid activities, conversations, or events because I don't feel mentally sharp enough to keep up.	0	1	3	4
My dull memory holds me back from doing things I would like to do.	0	1	3	4
My family complains that I'm too forgetful.	0	1	2	3
I have trouble going to sleep or staying asleep because of stressful thoughts.	0	1	2	3
I experience headaches, stomach pain, or digestive problems because of negativity.	0	1	2	3
Add the numbers you circled in each column.				

Now add the total for each column to get your score: _____

What Does Your Score Mean?

If your score is 12 or less, you're facing a MILD struggle with memory.
While you may occasionally misplace things or forget names, you're

committed to acquiring knowledge, learning new skills, and taking other steps to maintain a healthy mind. The remainder of this book is full of tips that can help you increase brain power and keep your mind sharp.

If your score is more than 13 and less than 21, you're facing a MODERATE struggle with memory. Although it may not always hold you back, forgetfulness, brain freeze, and fuzzy thinking has become a regular frustration for you. It's important that you use the strategies outlined in this chapter, as well as Chapters 7 and 9, in order to prevent it from getting worse.

If your score is more than 21, you have a SEVERE struggle with memory. While you may feel like your memory is a lost cause, there is hope. The strategies in this section will let you craft your own custom plan for reclaiming brain power. It's also a good idea to consult your doctor to see if any physical problems are contributing to your cloudy thinking.

✦

With your memory self-assessment complete, and a general idea of what you need to focus on, it's time to launch a highly practical and interactive section of my book. Beginning with this chapter, I'm going to introduce you to fast, fun, easy-to-follow tools that can help you improve your thinking: My step-by-step Memory Magic Plan.

According to medical experts, each new fact we learn will grow new dendrites, so we need to keep feeding our brains new information. My techniques will engage our brain cells as we memorize facts and acquire new information, learn to improve focus, and explore exercises that increase creativity, knowledge, and intuition.

At the end of the chapter you'll find "My Memory Magic

Planning Chart"—a tool you can fill in, enabling you to monitor your progress each week. I also encourage you to visit my online memory class at http://memorymastercourse.com.

Are you ready to get started? Here are the Memory Magic steps we'll cover in this chapter: (1) Acquiring Knowledge, (2) Building Skills, (3) Becoming More Social, and (4) Incorporating Brain Exercises.

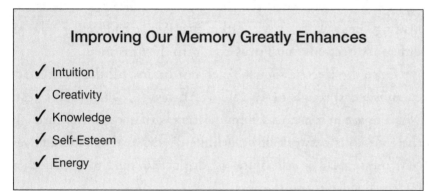

ACQUIRING KNOWLEDGE

It's powerful, mysterious, and more complex than any of today's most advanced computers. Of course I'm talking about the human brain, which controls the body's nervous system, processes incoming sensory impulses—sight, sound, smell, touch, taste—and is the center of reasoning, intellect, memory, consciousness, and emotions. The brain controls all behaviors, both conscious and subconscious. So how does it all work? More specifically, how do we receive information, learn, and acquire knowledge?

Everything we see, smell, hear, taste, and touch travels through our bodies in the form of electric signals, which pass from cell to cell until they reach our brains.[27] They enter at the base near the spinal cord, but must travel to our frontal lobe (behind the forehead) before reaching the place where rational, logical thinking takes place.[28] It's interesting to note that they first pass through the place where emotions are produced—our limbic system. According to clinical psychologist Dr. David Walton, our emotions are powerful at shaping our understanding, our ways of thinking, the decisions we make, and the habits or attitudes we adopt. "Cognitive science has repeatedly demonstrated the role that emotion plays in decision-making," he explains, "to the extent that if logic and feeling point in different directions, most people go with their instincts."[29]

Once the electric signals reach our brains, all the work is accomplished through nerve cells (or neurons), which never rest. Neurons are in constant communication with one another through the enormous network of branchlike dendrites that send and receive messages. The cells of the dendritic field "talk" to one another by releasing neurotransmitters.[30]

The junctions through which information passes from one neuron to another are called synapses, which can excite the body or inhibit it. In other words, they cause us to be stressed or to sleep; to be happy or to be sad. The neuron sends on the information it receives from all of its synapses—and ultimately affects our emotions, our behavior, our thinking . . . and how we learn and acquire knowledge.

As we learn, information enters our short-term memory first, and then some of it transfers later to long-term storage in our brain. Sleep is often important to transferring something from short- to long-term memory. Learning something new is often exciting for the learner. It can cause a rush of dopamine, which not only makes learning seem exciting but also makes us want to repeat the experience. Dopamine is also involved in experiences like love, addictive behaviors, and attention deficit disorder, among many other things.

There are eight key ways we acquire knowledge:

1. *Reading.* Do this every day and, most important, do it as a critical thinker.
2. *Writing.* Take notes. As you write something down, you're actually recording it in your own memory.
3. *Listening.* Close your mouth, open your ears, and hear what someone has to say.
4. *Observing.* Use all your senses and pay attention to what's happening around you.
5. *Experiencing.* Don't settle for someone else's opinion. Engage your mind and your senses and put knowledge into practice.
6. *Memorizing.* Learn something new, and then test it.
7. *Pondering.* Think deeply about things you've learned. Meditate on truths and commit them to memory.
8. *Reasoning.* Exercise the process by which we reason (called logic). This teaches us two things: how to derive a previously unknown truth from facts, and how *to be sure* what we think is true is really true.

How does any of this apply to improving our memory?

Each and every time we learn something new, our brains form new connections and neurons and make existing neural pathways stronger or weaker. Some experts call these changes "plasticity" in the brain. Dendrites in our neurons get signals from other dendrites, and the signals travel along the axon, which connects them to other neurons and dendrites. These signals travel fast, often in only fractions of a second, and many of the signals are sent without the brain being aware of the action. Our brains will continue changing right up until the end of our lives, so the more we learn along the way, the more our brains will change.

Memorizing New Facts and New Information

✓ Improves cognitive abilities

✓ Slows down the aging process in the brain

✓ Increases brain mass

✓ Stimulates neurogenesis—the growth and development of nervous tissue

✓ Promotes neuroplasticity

→ **Discover more ways to acquire knowledge. Turn to the Appendix: "Ultimate Brain Games and Memory Exercises."**

LEARNING NEW SKILLS

As we've discovered so far, it's essential that we use our brains by challenging ourselves mentally. Learning a new skill over a long period of time is another important step in our brain-boosting strategy. Not only is it good for our minds, practicing a new skill increases the density of our myelin, the white matter in our brains that helps improve performance on a number of tasks. What's more, learning new skills stimulates neurons in the brain, which form more neural pathways, enabling electrical impulses to travel faster across them. The combination of these two things helps us learn better, and it ultimately improves our memory.

Myelin makes the signals in our neurons move faster, and

when you learn new things, especially at older ages, it helps more myelin get onto our nerve axons so that our brains are more connected and feel like they work faster and better. Myelin works especially well when a new experience is repeated multiple times, like when we practice something or repeat it every day or every few days.

Here's a trick to sharpening your thinking: Shock your brain and recharge your mind by learning something entirely new, something that seems out of character for you. In other words, if you're creative, learn a mechanical skill (such as basic auto maintenance). If you're a scientist, pick up a paintbrush and let your inner artist create. Refreshing our minds pulls us out of a cognitive rut and enables us to think differently.

Boosting your memory by learning a new skill should be a fun, motivating experience. As a way to customize a plan that will work best for you, follow each of these steps and jot down your thoughts in the spaces provided. Let's begin.

SKILL-BUILDER SELF-ASSESSMENT

Step 1: Identify Your Interests

First, look inward and think about your interests, desires, and the kinds of topics you'd like to explore. On the left side of the box on the following page, brainstorm as many subjects you can fit in the space. Don't think too hard about them. Just let the ideas flow. On the right side, jot down the best way to learn these skills, if it will be easy or time-consuming, and if there's an expense involved. (For example, if it requires taking a class and if it involves a fee.) I filled out the first one for you.

Skills That Interest Me	How I Can Acquire these Skills
Learn the basics of ballroom dancing	Take a class Easy/Time-Consuming/$$$
_____	_____ Easy/Time-Consuming/$$$
_____	_____ Easy/Time-Consuming/$$$
_____	_____ Easy/Time-Consuming/$$$
_____	_____ Easy/Time-Consuming/$$$
_____	_____ Easy/Time-Consuming/$$$
_____	_____ Easy/Time-Consuming/$$$
_____	_____ Easy/Time-Consuming/$$$
_____	_____ Easy/Time-Consuming/$$$
_____	_____ Easy/Time-Consuming/$$$
_____	_____ Easy/Time-Consuming/$$$

Step 2: Pinpoint Your Personality

I'm often described as (circle only one pair of words and phrases):

Mechanically Minded/Technical
Inventive/ Problem-Solver
Creative/Artistic
Outdoor Enthusiast/Adventurous
Athletic/Competitive
Scientific/Mathematical
Investigative/Fact-Finder
Legal-Minded/Detail-Oriented
People Person/Communicator
Planner/Organizer

Step 3: Double-Check Your Wiring

Let's zero in on how you learn best. Respond to the following statements.

Ways I prefer to acquire information include:

Intensive reading and research
Attending a class
Hearing a motivational speaker
Online and with discussion groups
Through the arts, including music and the visual arts
Using experiential methods: hands-on learning
Using scientific methods
Time spent alone in deep reflection and meditation

Other things that help me grow include:

1.
2.
3.

Things that block growth include:

1.
2.
3.

My top ten sources of inspiration include (you can list people, books, movies, talks, journeys . . .):

1.
2.

3.

4.

5.

6.

7.

8.

9.

10.

Step 4: Set Some Goals

There are three things you've got to remember about setting a skill-building goal: It must be *concrete, measurable,* and *attainable.*

A concrete goal is one you can put into words. A vague desire to "learn a new language" is not very concrete. But "take an online course in Swedish for three months" is a solid goal. Goals are most concrete when written down.

A measurable goal is one that allows you to see progress. "Learn to speak Swedish" is tough to measure. But "learn to speak fifteen basic Swedish phrases in three months" allows you to mark your progress.

An attainable goal is one that can reasonably be completed. "Speak fluent Swedish in three months" is both concrete and measurable, but hardly attainable. "Be able to engage in fifteen basic conversations in Swedish in three months" is a goal that meets all three criteria.

Now it's time to set some skill-building goals that will challenge your mind and boost your memory. At this point in our exercise, you should have a pretty good idea of your personality and learning preferences. So with this information in mind, go back to Step 1 and identify three goals you'd like to pursue over the next twelve months. (Give yourself three to four months to accomplish each one.) Once you've made a decision, jot down your choices, along with your plan, in the spaces provided.

Next step: Engage in some new skills and challenge your mind.

A New Skill to Acquire	How I Will Acquire It	How Long It Will Take	End Result
Skill #1: _____			
Skill #2: _____			
Skill #3: _____			

→ **Discover more skill-building ideas. Turn to the Appendix: "Ultimate Brain Games and Memory Exercises."**

BECOMING MORE SOCIAL

As I pointed out in Chapter 5, the happiest people are those who connect daily with friends and family. They are also the smartest.

Author Oscar Ybarra, Ph.D., and his colleagues at the University of Michigan explored the possibility that social interaction improves mental functioning. In a series of related studies, they tested the participants' level of cognitive functioning, comparing it to the frequency of participants' social interactions.[31] They found that people who engaged in social interaction displayed higher levels of cognitive performance than the control group. Social interaction aided intellectual performance.

"Social interaction," the authors suggest, "helps to exercise people's minds. People reap cognitive benefits from socializing." They speculate that social interaction exercises cognitive processes that are measured on intellectual tasks. "It is possible," the authors conclude, "that as people engage socially and mentally with others, they receive relatively immediate cognitive boosts."[32]

On the flip side, cognition declines if we become isolated and lonely and, sadly, a growing number of us feel overlooked and alone—from Generation Z to the senior crowd. In fact, research has found that loneliness is currently "the silent epidemic" worldwide. In Great Britain, for example, more than nine million people say they "often or always feel lonely," according to a 2017 report published by the Jo Cox Commission on Loneliness.[33] The issue prompted Prime Minister Theresa May to appoint a Minister for Loneliness.

"For far too many people, loneliness is the sad reality of modern life," Mrs. May said in a statement. "I want to confront this challenge for our society and for all of us to take action to address the loneliness endured by the elderly, by caregivers, by those who have lost loved ones—people who have no one to talk to or share their thoughts and experiences with."[34]

Imagine that—even though we live in a time when those in both advanced and emerging nations are glued to their smartphones and are more connected than at any other time in history—loneliness is an epidemic. That's because there is a big difference between being connected and belonging. And as leaders like Mrs. May and researchers know, being social and feeling a sense of belonging is what we all desire. Without it, we suffer.

Socializing is another step toward boosting our brain power, and the sky's the limit on how we can connect with others. Here are some of my favorite ideas.

+ Use technology to your advantage. Hop on Skype or Facetime and reach out to family and friends who live in another state—or another part of the world.
+ If you're single or widowed, don't just sit at home alone. Find a friend and socialize: Go to the movies; visit a museum; start a book club; volunteer together.

- Walk through your neighborhood and make a point of stopping to say hello to people you meet.
- My wife, Lynn, and I love to babysit our grandkids. We have fun with them, testing their memory and playing brain-boosting games with them.
- Sign up for a class at your local recreation center, library, or university.
- Join a church, synagogue, or temple, and start attending services and events there.
- Sing in a choir or play music in a group.
- Participate in a neighborhood or community group.
- Start a game night and play cards or board games with others.
- Exercise with a friend by walking, swimming, or going to the gym together.
- Play a group sport like lawn bowling, golf, or croquet.
- Discover new wines with a friend. If you don't drink, explore coffees or teas.

INCORPORATING BRAIN EXERCISES

Brain-training apps for smartphones are a big business, and the options are seemingly endless in today's marketplace. But do they actually work? The jury is still out, with some researchers claiming they do improve the brain's executive functions—for example, the ability to pay attention, organize, and plan. These same researchers say brain-training apps enhance the working memory and processing speed of young people, as well as the cognitive health of seniors. But on the flip side of the debate, some experts insist that no such benefits exist. One study monitored the brain activity, cognitive skills, and decision-making abilities of young adults, only to conclude that brain-training games "do not boost cognition"[35] and that there is no effect on decision-making.

Here's what I've learned, as well as what many researchers have proven: We can boost our brain's performance with memory regimens that incorporate physical fitness, diet, socialization, education, as well as mental exercises that target specific goals so we can attain tangible results. In other words, the kind of mind-body-emotional holistic approach that has transformed my life—and that I'm sharing with you in these very pages!

"If you're looking to improve your cognitive self, instead of playing a video game or playing a brain-training test for an hour, go for a walk, go for a run, socialize with a friend," says Bobby Stojanoski, Ph.D., a research scientist in the Brain and Mind Institute at Canada's Western University.[36] "Sleep better, exercise regularly, eat better, education is great—that's the sort of thing we should be focused on."[37]

We've already discussed the benefits of acquiring knowledge, building skills, and becoming more social. Now it's time to explore brain-boosting exercises that work. I have included here effective mnemonic devices (memory-building techniques) that are fun and easy to apply, yet aren't just meant for entertainment. My list is designed to give you a great mental workout and improve your thinking in a short period of time. On the pages that follow (and in the Appendix), you'll find the best of the best: dozens of acronyms and memory devices, right along with mental exercises and little-known tricks that will improve your cognitive fitness. At the end of this chapter (as well as the next one), I've provided "My Memory Magic Planning Chart." This is your place to develop your own weekly brain-boosting regimen.

One last thing before we dive in. I want you to promise me two things: (1) You won't defeat yourself before you even get started, thinking, *My memory is too shot to do any of this.* (2) You won't allow yourself to feel overwhelmed by all of the options I'm throwing at you. Look, if I can do this, you can too. (Go back and reread my story in Part One for some inspiration.)

The fact is, the capacity to learn and to remember things is quite similar among moderately healthy individuals because our brains really aren't all that different. We just have to exercise them. And the trick to maximizing the effectiveness of any memory technique rests in the information we are plugging into our brains.

✓ **Memory Trick #1:** Acquire knowledge and skills and memorize information that is fun to learn and that interests you.

✓ **Memory Trick #2:** Incorporate memory aids (descriptive or rhyming words, memories, etc.) that are creative, positive, vivid . . . and even amusing and silly.

Techniques for Memorizing Lists

Here are some of my favorite mnemonic devices. Each one will enable you to retain and recall lists, blocks of information, and reading material. At first, these methods may seem silly or strange. But once you grasp each concept, you'll discover their effectiveness and you'll sharpen your thinking. The key to sharpening your mind and improving your memory is practice.

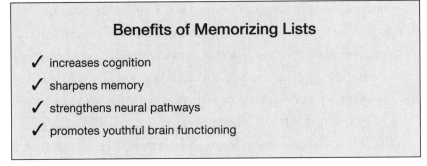

Benefits of Memorizing Lists

✓ increases cognition
✓ sharpens memory
✓ strengthens neural pathways
✓ promotes youthful brain functioning

Visual Link Method

With this technique you can change abstract facts into mental pictures that are easy to remember. Essentially, you "link" and connect items in memory that may not be related. Here's a demonstration of the Visual Link Method using the following thirteen random words and phrases: *(1) car, (2) cinder block, (3) bear, (4) potato, (5) swimming pool, (6) taxicab, (7) priest, (8) spaghetti, (9) ping-pong ball, (10) butterfly, (11) Coke can, (12) table, (13) triangle.*

Let's say you need to memorize this list in this order. First, *link* the thirteen words together with a story. And the more outrageous the story, the more likely you'll remember it. Second, it's *very important* to *visualize* your story as you ponder it.

Here's a memory story I created:

I was backing my CAR out of the driveway when, all of a sudden, I hit a CINDER BLOCK. I got out of my car and was amazed to see that the cinder block fell onto a BEAR's big toe. The angry bear was eating a POTATO and threw it at me. The potato went sailing into my neighbors SWIMMING POOL. When I walked toward the pool, I noticed it was empty—yet there was a TAXICAB in the middle of the pool. As I looked closer, I saw a PRIEST sitting in the backseat of the car eating SPAGHETTI. But he wasn't eating spaghetti and meatballs. Instead, he was eating spaghetti and PING-PONG BALLS. He stuck his head out the back window and had a ping-pong ball in his opened mouth. When he spit it out, it turned into a beautiful BUTTERFLY. The butterfly flew onto a COKE CAN that was setting on an unusual-looking glass TABLE, which was shaped like a TRIANGLE!

Most people who hear this story just one time instantly remember all thirteen words! Once again, the key is to visualize everything happening in the story.

Acronyms

I started using acronyms way back in elementary school, and I've never stopped since. This is an old-school memory device that works. (I've even made up several of my own through the years.) So what is an acronym? Technically, it's a word formed from the first letters of a list of words, or as Webster's defines it, "An abbreviation (such as FBI) formed from initial letters." As far as I'm concerned, the rules can be bent for a memory technique, so any catchy or invented combination of letters (or even a phrase) that can easily be remembered is an acronym. Each letter signals an item we need to remember. To create one, simply take the list of words, phrases, or facts that you want to memorize and order them so that the initial letters of each word spell a real or made-up word.

Here are some examples along with practical ways to use them:

Acronym Basics: Use Them to . . .

Remember Lists

Example: The Five Great Lakes

HOMES

Huron Ontario Michigan Erie Superior

Spell Words

Example: Arithmetic

A Rat In Tom's House Might

Eat Tom's Ice Cream

Memorize a Series or a Pattern

Example: Musical Scale

EGBDF

Every Good Boy Does Fine

Memorize a Collection of Items

Example: Eight Bones of the Human Skull

FOES TP

Frontal Occipital Ethmoid Sphenoid plus two Temporal and two Parietal

✓ **Memory Trick #3:** For especially difficult items to memorize (such as scientific and medical terms), incorporate a vivid story or memory with your acronym. Using the fourth example above—the eight bones of the human skull—I tied my acronym to a childhood memory: When I was a kid, my brother and I once made teepees by propping up two playing cards. We created a "control center" with EIGHT teepees. And then came the test of our NUMB-SKULLS. We would take turns pulling a "sock brainwave" through each teepee, ultimately knocking them down until ONE was left standing. My brother, being my FOE, destroyed the last TP. Since it was made using TWO cards, I will always remember we have two TEMPORAL bones and two PARIETAL bones in our skulls. I know what you're thinking: *How can this silly story aid memory?* Remember what I said in Trick #2? Incorporate memory aids that are creative, positive, vivid . . . and even amusing and silly. These types of memories are fun and stick with us, just as this one helps me remember the eight bones of our skulls.

Peg Anchor Systems

With this effective technique, you associate items you want to remember with certain images in a prearranged order. The system gets its name from key words that act as mental pegs—what I call "anchors"—on which you hang information you're committing to memory. It's a good way to begin if you need to memorize a list of ten to twenty things. This method has helped me memorize things like 52 playing cards, 50 states, 109 chemical elements, etc. (I even came up with my own version that has many more anchors.) I can't stress it enough: Once you get the hang of this technique, you'll find that it's highly useful. Anchor words can help you remember lists of items or errands and daily activities. It requires remembering in two distinct stages: One involving the right hemisphere and the other involving the left.[38]

Unlike the Visual Link Method that we discussed above, a peg is not dependent on retrieving an item in sequence. You can access any piece of information on the list without having to work your way through the whole thing. It is, however, a bit more complicated to learn at first.

There are a variety of Peg System options—from very basic to extremely complex. In the paragraphs that follow, I'll guide you through the Rhyming Peg System (one of the most popular techniques), and then I invite you to flip over to the Appendix: "Ultimate Brain Games and Memory Exercises"—and I'll show you another peg exercise, as well as one that I customized.

Rhyming Peg

Here's the basic idea: You construct a number of anchors using words that rhyme or that sound alike. Studies have shown that our ability to recall information is significantly improved by using rhyming words. This method is useful for short lists and is quite effective for lists containing as many as twenty items. You begin by associating a rhyming word with the numbers from 1 to 20. Let's explore the following example.

1. Sun	2. Shoe	3. Tree	4. Door	5. Hive
6. Sticks	7. Heaven	8. Plate	9. Sign	10. Hen

- Using the list of ten words above, say each rhyme out loud: "One, sun . . . two, shoe . . . three, tree . . ."

- Do it again, but this time picture the item that the anchor word represents. See it vividly. For example, imagine the bright, warm sun; envision a brown leather shoe; see the expansive shady tree and a bright red door . . . and so on.

- Practice saying the list over and over during the next few days until it becomes permanently fixed in your long-term memory. Once you've formed an association between the numbers and the words that rhyme with them, you've constructed your anchors. At this point, you'll be able to think of an anchor and instantly remember the image that's linked to it.

- Finally, test your memory by imagining the anchor words in place of the numbers and randomly hop around the list: Jump over to two, and then to seven, and on to one. Eventually, you won't have to say the numbers to recall the words. That's because they rhyme, which has enabled you to fix them in your memory.

If this feels a bit like the technique I taught you with the Visual Link Method, as well as with acronyms, you're right. Using a story will not only help you commit anchor words to memory, it will enable you to recall them very quickly and easily.

Once the peg words are permanently assigned to their numerical counterpart, you can associate the items you want to remember to the peg word image. Not only will you be able to recall the list, you will also know the exact numerical position of each item in the list![39]

→ **Discover more techniques for memorizing lists. Turn to the Appendix: "Ultimate Brain Games and Memory Exercises."**

Techniques for Remembering Names, Faces, and Places

Freshly brewed coffee. A big tub of hot, buttered popcorn. The orange-golden glow of a sunset. The soothing sounds of Brahms Symphony No. 4. Just saying each description conjures up so many emotions and memories in my mind—and I bet yours too. Do you know why? Because each one engages our senses. And as we've discussed earlier, we can fix data and information in our memory by taking three key steps:

Tap in to our senses. Incorporating all our five senses into memory techniques can stimulate the brain and improve our ability to recall information. The most powerful senses for recall are sight, sound, and smell.

Use mental images. Names and numbers are hard to remember because they're abstract and our brains can't easily latch onto them. But our brains store and recall images much more easily.

Create word pictures. Visualize the spelling of a word in your head, then try to think of any other words that begin (or end) with the same two letters.

So, let's get practical. We'll use Amy as our example. (She's the young English teacher we met at the beginning of this chapter.)

Amy shows us how she mixes the three memory tricks above with other techniques, such as the Peg System, in order to help her remember names, faces, and places.

How to Make Sense of Abstract Names

Technique #1: Engage Your Senses

First, Amy turns a name into a sound and an image. For example, let's say one of her students walks up to her and says, "Hi, I'm Isabella." Amy immediately clues in to something that's unique about the girl's name, and then she engages her own five senses, conjuring up images, sounds, smells, etc. Doing this enables Amy to turn something abstract (a name) into something memorable (an image). So, in the case of Isabella, Amy envisions a bell and the high-pitched sound it makes as it rings. She then associates the image with Isabella's name and the sound with the girl's high-pitched voice.

Then, the second step is to peg (or anchor) that image onto the place where she will remember it. Amy anchors Isabella's name, as well as the image and sound of a bell ringing, to the second-row seat where the girl sits during third-period English. (Amy literally imagines a bell sitting in the chair in front of her!)

Finally, Amy animates the images. The more animated and vivid you can make these images, the better. Doing this creates stronger, novel connections in your brain between that word or number and an image. In this case, Amy imagines a bell ringing each time she sees Isabella.

Technique #2: Make a Common Connection

Here's another technique Amy uses to remember a name: She often associates the name of an acquaintance—or a student she meets for the first time—with either (1) someone she knows personally, or with (2) a famous name. For example, when she was introduced to a student named Ricardo, she associated the boy's name with the actor Ricardo Montalban.

So, here's the trick: The second you meet someone, think about a famous person (or someone you know personally) who shares that person's first name and who, perhaps, looks somewhat like them. Once you make the association, it will be locked into your memory.

Technique #3: Repeat a New Name

Repetition helps you remember. Each time you repeat a new name, it helps to lock it into your memory. Before Amy leaves a student she just met, the young teacher makes sure she verbalizes the person's name. Simply saying, "Goodbye, Lucas," or, "I'll see you tomorrow, Sofia," helps her to cement the name in her mind. What's more, it gives her a much better chance of remembering it the next time she sees the student.

The fact is, we can't memorize something if we don't repeat it. Repeating a person's name aloud so we can hear it and visualizing it so we see it gives us an audiovisual aid to help us retain names and faces.

Technique #4: Observe Someone's Face When You Meet Them

In addition to remembering each student's name, Amy strives to remember their face. She makes an effort to study each one as they talk, taking note of particularly unique features and mentally repeating their name. She observes the shape of their face, the size of their nose, unusual eye color, their hairstyle, their smile. In other words, Amy pauses and takes the time to *see* each student she meets. Taking the time to link their physical features to their name not only enables the busy teacher to remember their face and details of their lives, it helps her to make a personal connection with the people she encounters.

How to Remember Directions and Places

Amy grew up in Chicago—the third largest city in the United States—so she knows the importance of being good with directions and having the ability to quickly recall places in and around the city. But it hasn't come easy for her. In all honesty, Amy doesn't naturally possess a keen sense of direction.

Yet instead of getting frustrated, she decided to get smart! The same power of observation and sensory tricks she applies to remembering names and faces enables her to recall directions and places.

First, she strives to have a deep interest in the places she travels to. Just as she studies a person's face, she has learned to *see* her environment. Amy takes note of the direction of the streets she travels, paying attention to the landmarks, the twists and turns of the road, and even the natural objects along the way.

Next, she nurtures place-memory. Each time she rides the Chicago "L" (the city's rapid transit system) or walks along city blocks, she commits her path to memory, noting the landmarks and the general directions and relative positions. With each step, she tries to see how many things she can remember. When she returns home, she retraces the path in her mind, quizzing herself to see how many landmarks she can remember.

Here are three strategies she employs:

1. *Use a mental map.* Whether you're heading off on a trip to a new place, or an appointment in an unfamiliar part of town, study a physical map first . . . and then create a mental one. *Do this before you head out the door.* In your mind, visualize key landmarks: distinctive buildings, a tree-lined street, a theater or a library. Recall how the primary highways and boulevards run from north to south, or east to west. With a clear

idea where the main roads are and how they branch out into side streets, think about the direction you will travel, as well as where you can turn in case you do get lost. These simple steps will save you from headaches later and will help you to recall the location of a place when the pressure is on.

2. *Use rhymes or songs.* Here's a way to remember street names and directions: Create short rhyming sentences out of the street names, and then connect them to a story. Remember: the more imaginative the story, the better. Also, try singing them to the melody of your favorite song.

For example, here's how I make my way to my favorite seafood hangout in Philadelphia. I sing it to the theme music to *Gilligan's Island:*

> *Let's head downtown and have a round at my Chart House seafood spot / I'll make a turn and won't get burned as I walk the Delaware dock / I'll find the sign and be on time at my 555 Columbus rock."*

Here's a story Amy used to locate a bookstore in an unfamiliar part of Chicago:

> I trek through the urban jungle, upstream on the chilly **North Michigan Ave.**, past the three monuments to wealth and royalty: The **Conrad**, the **Omni**, and **Saks Fifth Avenue**. I cruise through the **Peninsula**, escape the **Nordstrom Rack** . . . and head **West** on a way that flows **East** through the Windy City: **East Chicago Ave.** I swim past a flood of commuters and finally reach my happy place: **The Loyola University Bookstore.**

3. *Use a link.* The more you're able to link items, the more you'll be able to learn and recall information. And the more you can relate

certain information with what you already know, the more you'll remember information. The key is to attach one direction to another. In other words, if you already know how to get to the main road, just connect the side streets by linking them through your mind, whether you turn left or right.[40]

Amy strives to employ her senses too. She associates an address or the name of a boulevard or highway with mental pictures that evoke images, sounds, and smells. For example, Chicago's "Highway 41" leads to downtown's "front lawn": Millennium Park. For Amy, that highway triggers the "thousands" of images she cherishes from a happy childhood spent exploring the park. (Millennium Park is often referred to as Chicago's "front lawn.")

Math Games to Sharpen Your Thinking

Math and memory go together like baseball and apple pie!

Here's a simple exercise that I like—one that you can do right away. It's called *Add 3 Minus 7*. Here's the idea: All you do is pick any three-digit number, and then you add three to that digit three times. Next, you "minus" seven from the new number seven times. Got it? Your goal is to repeat the process at least five times, and then you pick a new three-digit number the next time. You can also start with a four-digit number and use other numbers to play with. For example, if you're really ambitious—and want a serious challenge—you could start with 7,777 and add seven, seven times . . . and minus fourteen, fourteen times. Whew—that's tough, but it will give your brain a great workout!

This brain exercise also strengthens your working memory because of the amount of detail you need to hold in mind to complete it.

→ **Sharpen your thinking with more math games and exercises. Turn to the Appendix: Ultimate Brain Games and Memory Exercises.**

✓ **Memory Trick #4: Do Math in Your Head** Figure out problems without the aid of pencil, paper, or computer; you can make this more difficult—and athletic—by walking at the same time.

MY MEMORY MAGIC PLANNING CHART

Enhance Memory and Sharpen Focus

Day	How I Will Acquire Knowledge	How I Will Build New Skills	How I Will Socialize More	How I Will Incorporate Brain Exercises
Sunday				
Monday				
Tuesday				
Wednesday				
Thursday				
Friday				
Saturday				

LET'S TAKE OUR MINDS TO THE NEXT LEVEL

In tandem with a memory-boosting system is an exercise regimen designed to get our hearts pumping, our muscles moving, and our bodies toned. The next chapter offers a plan that you can personalize and apply to your own life.

MY MEMORY MAGIC PLAN: AT-A-GLANCE STEPS

Brain-Booster No. 1: Enhance Memory and Sharpen Focus

- Take My Memory Self-Assessment
- Take My Skill-Builder Self-Assessment
- Customize your own Memory Magic Plan that involves the following steps: (1) Acquiring Knowledge, (2) Building Skills, (3) Becoming More Social, and (4) Incorporating Brain Exercises

Brain-Booster No. 2: Rev Up Energy and Self-Esteem

Toning Your Body as You Boost Your Brain

It was torture. Gut-wrenching, muscle-depleting, lose-your-lunch torture.

The world-famous Chicago Marathon is a race only for the strong of heart. Clint was strong, no doubt about it. He played football and wrestled in high school. In college, he switched to lacrosse. But a marathon—at his age?!

This is insane! Clint told himself as he maintained a steady pace with thousands of other runners. It was his first competition and his inaugural trek down Lake Shore Drive.

How did I get talked into this?

Actually, the forty-eight-year-old airline mechanic knew the answer to that question: his wife.

"This is a once-in-a-lifetime thing," she had told him several months earlier, desperately trying to convince him to take on this challenge. "You trained hard and lost all that weight. Now you're like this totally hot stud! You're stronger, smarter—you can do this."

"But I'm not a runner," Clint argued. "I'm a mechanic from Omaha, Nebraska."

"You're an athlete from Omaha," his wife clarified, "and you're in the best shape of your life. Imagine finishing in record time? Imagine the bragging rights?!"

"Imagine just finishing," he said. "That's all I can hope for."

Even though Clint put up a good fight, deep down inside he loved his wife's support—and he knew she was right. Ever since he got serious about improving his health, she had been cheering him along, challenging him to take on dreams he had never thought he could achieve. This had boosted his self-esteem—as had seeing some big results: His mind was sharper and his body was healthier. In the past, some of his coworkers had talked endlessly about watching the Chicago Marathon. So Clint decided to train for it.

"Really think I can do this?" he asked.

His wife just smiled. "I know you can."

So here he was eight months later. To Clint's surprise, a wide range of people can enter the marathon. You must be at least sixteen years old and be able to run the 26.2-mile course in 6 hours and 30 minutes. That's it. Yet the Omaha native knew that not everyone should enter—and he had plenty of doubts about his own chances.

Three-quarters of the way into the race, Clint continued his steady run to Grant Park, enduring the grueling punishment of what many consider the pinnacle of achievement for elite athletes and everyday runners alike. Three hours into his run, Clint became even more convinced of what he knew all along: Running was invented by deranged, Groot-like aliens who gave up guarding the galaxy so they could torture unsuspecting airline mechanics! (Clint was a big sci-fi fan, especially the *Guardians of the Galaxy* movies.)

Three hours turned into four; four turned into four and a half. Before he knew it, Clint could see the finish line. *I'm nearly there! I can't believe it. I'm going to finish this race—and I'm going to do it faster than I ever imagined.*

Suddenly, though, Clint's mind began to play tricks on him. Waves of nausea lapped at his tonsils. He imagined himself morphing into a human geyser and erupting like Old Faithful—with bits of breakfast burrito and orange droplets of Gatorade raining down on the crowd!

Push through, he told himself. *I can do this. I'm going to finish— with a personal best!*

As he kept running, his inner athlete took over. Head erect, legs pounding, arms pumping in the cool October air. He was nearing the finish line, mentally and physically committed.

And then something amazing happened. The nausea disappeared, and he focused on the prize: bragging rights . . . the affirmation of his wife.

Minutes later, he crossed the finish line!

Clint's time: Four hours, forty-seven minutes.

His wife cheered as he raised his arms high in the air. A big smile stretched across his face as he achieved a personal victory.

"At first, it felt so insane to even be doing this," he told his wife and friends. "But I actually did it. And now I feel as if I can do anything. As we exercise our minds and our bodies, we become *super*-human!"

✦

We head to the gym to give our bodies a workout, and we engage in memory exercises to stimulate the growth of cells in our brain. But as I discovered more than a decade ago—and as people like Clint are proving—we can boost our brain power, strengthen our bodies, *and* transform our lives through a combination of *mind-body* exercises. As we employ this powerful duo, we become healthier, our confidence soars, and our thinking becomes much sharper.

Clint summed it up best: "We become *super*-human!"

According to my friend and colleague, Dr. Daniel Amen, aerobic and anaerobic workouts have positive effects on brain function on multiple fronts, ranging from the molecular to the behavioral level. "Those who exercise for just twenty minutes a day improve information processing and memory functions."

Feeding our minds information while doing physical exercise makes a good thing even better. It increases blood flow to our brains *and* increases nitric oxide levels. As our heart rate increases, more oxygen is pumped to the brain—right along with nitric oxide. Our bodies naturally produce this molecule, which relaxes the inner muscles of the blood vessels, causing them to widen and increase circulation. Blood, nutrients, and oxygen travel throughout our bodies more effectively and efficiently, helping us to feel better and to think better, as well. The better we feel and the sharper we think, the more we can learn and commit information to our long-term memory— which, in turn, grows more brain cells . . . making us smarter.

According to Dr. Amen, consistent, daily exercise has so many benefits: It increases antioxidant activity, and it helps to reduce the breakdown of nitric oxide caused by free radicals, as well as disorders that lead to memory loss, such as diabetes and cardiovascular disease. In general, anything that is good for our hearts is great for our brains.

Current research from University of California at Los Angeles (UCLA) reveals that a combination of mental and physical exercise increases growth factors in the brain—making it easier for it to grow new neuronal connections. In other words, mind-body exercise stimulates brain plasticity by sparking the growth of new connections between cells in a wide array of important cortical regions of the brain.

Here's another way this exercise duo boosts our brain: We

EXERCISE IS GOOD FOR THE BRAIN

✓ It enhances the effects of helpful brain chemicals and reduces stress hormones
✓ It plays an important role in neuroplasticity—the brain's capacity to change throughout our lifetime, growing stronger and more powerful
✓ It aids the bodily release of a plethora of hormones, each of which participates in aiding and providing a nourishing environment for the growth of brain cells

experience the euphoric effects of the "runner's high." It's what pushed Clint over the finish line at the Chicago Marathon, and it's often what I experience during vigorous workouts.

Author and medical expert Julian Whitaker, M.D., explains it this way: "Ever notice how exercise puts you in a better mood? It's not just your imagination," he says. "Exercise stimulates your brain to produce hormones called endorphins, natural painkillers and mood enhancers. That is why exercise produces such a wonderful 'natural high.'"[41]

Researchers claim this euphoric state can also be triggered by endocannabinoids (ECs)—small molecules that, believe it or not, are similar to the cannabinoids found in marijuana. These naturally produced chemical compounds in our bodies affect many important functions, including how a person feels, moves, and reacts. According to Dr. Scott Weiss, a board-certified athletic trainer and licensed physical therapist in New York City, "Combine ECs with other enzymes that get released [during exercise] and that breaks the barrier, that's really what gives someone the runner's high."[42]

Though the high isn't limited to runners, it's not something someone doing, say, sets of squats and pull-ups is likely to experience; the key is duration. Runners tend to spend more time training for long-distance races, including marathons, thus the greater association between the high and running.[43]

So we know that getting consistent daily exercise is an essential brain-booster. But what's the big deal about runner's high, and how can this euphoric state improve our health? Researchers from the University of Iowa claim that runner's high has the potential to promote heart health through the release of stress. In addition, those who achieve runner's high experience more speed, strength, and overall better performance.

Mind-body exercises can unlock the antidepressant effects along with more cell growth in the hippocampus—an area of the brain responsible for learning and memory—and they can also enhance cognitive function. Therefore, the best brain health workouts involve those that integrate different parts of the brain such as coordination, rhythm, and strategy. It not only strengthens our hearts, lowers blood pressure, improves muscle tone and reduces body fat, but it also reduces stress and turns negativity into positive energy!

Now that you know the benefits, as well as what's going on in your mind and your body, it's time to get started customizing a brain-fitness plan that will work best for you.

In the paragraphs that follow, I'll show you key ways to tone your body as you boost your brain, and I'll continue to spell out the benefits along the way. A daily memory regimen in tandem with physical exercise can transform our minds, our bodies, and our overall health. The more we exercise, the more we're able to think clearly, feel alert and energetic, and have a markedly increased sense of well-being.

Remember to work with your health care professional to make sure you are incorporating these exercises in your life in a way that is most beneficial to you.

EXERCISE RELEASES MOOD ENHANCERS

✓ People who exercise regularly get a positive boost in mood and self-esteem.

✓ When we exercise, our bodies release chemicals called endorphins. These endorphins give us positive feelings that energize our bodies and give us a sense of well-being.

✓ One word of caution: Each individual has a different reaction to stress. Therefore, it is essential that we customize a plan for defeating it, utilizing different measures to overcome different levels of stress.

LAUNCHING AEROBIC AND ANAEROBIC EXERCISE

The fact is, our bodies are made to be active. The harder we work them and the better the nutrients we put into them, the leaner, stronger, and more energetic they will become. In fact, the chemicals produced during moderate exercise can enhance the function of the immune system and train our bodies to deal with stress under controlled circumstances.

Here are the two types of exercise that we need to incorporate into our daily lives:

Aerobic Activity. The technical definition is "training with oxygen." In other words, an activity that gets your heart pumping and air flowing through your body: walking, hiking, jogging, swimming, bicycling, or cross-country skiing. The benefits are indisputable:

✓ Our heart is strengthened
✓ Blood pressure is lowered
✓ Metabolism is improved
✓ Fat stores are burned after 20–30 minutes of sustained activity
✓ Endorphins and other feel-good hormones are released

Anaerobic Exercise. This means "training without oxygen," and it involves all forms of high-intensity activity that are engaged for short periods of time. Examples include sprinting, resistance training (working out with weights), powerlifting, tennis, racquetball . . . and any other sport you can think of that causes fatigue to the muscles with harder but shorter bursts of energy. During anaerobic exercise, our cardiovascular system has a challenging time delivering the necessary levels of oxygen to our muscles fast enough. And since muscles require air to maintain prolonged exertion, anaerobic exercises can only continue for short periods of time. Why is it important for overall good health? Resistance training, for example, provides these benefits:

✓ We improve muscle strength, which enhances other athletic pursuits.
✓ It builds and maintains a lean, toned body.
✓ It enhances weight loss.
✓ We're able to fight stress through vigorous exercise.

Mixed in with physical exercise is proper breathing. Not only is this a crucial step as we work out, it also helps us manage stress. So when that pang of anxiety strikes and our hearts begins to race, we can take a simple step that can help quiet our minds, calm our emotions, and fuel our bodies.

◆ Breathe in slowly to the count of six and breathe out slowly to the count of six. Do this for five minutes; gradually increase to twenty minutes over time. The point is to slow your heart rate and reduce the pace at which stress hormones are flying through your system.
◆ While focusing on each breath, remind yourself that the anxiety you're feeling is a chemical response.[44]
◆ Repeat some phrases, verses, or prayers: "Relax and live in truth, not fear."

Deep breathing is helpful in interrupting irrational thoughts. But the key is to take long, steady breaths from the diaphragm. This slows down your heart rate, lowers blood pressure, and helps your body use oxygen more efficiently. It also has a calming effect. Not only do our lungs supply red blood cells with fresh oxygen—enabling normal cell function and proper metabolism—they also rid our bodies of harmful waste products such as carbon dioxide. We'll discuss this in detail in Chapter 10.

JIM KAROL'S WEEKLY BRAIN-BOOSTING EXERCISE PLAN

Exercise on a Stationary Bike Five Days a Week

▶ Begin with a 30-minute workout, gradually increasing it to 60 minutes.

▶ Keep a moderate pace and burn those calories. According to Harvard Health, a 155-pound person will burn about 520 calories per hour of bicycling at a moderate pace.

▶ The longer your workouts, the greater the heart benefits. In order to achieve weight loss and cardio benefits, it's important to elevate your heart rate at a steady pace. Work out within your target heart-rate range, which is 50 to 85 percent of your maximum heart rate. Here's how you can calculate this: Subtract your age from 220, and then multiply that number by both 0.50 and 0.85. This is your target heart rate range.

▶ As you pedal, exercise your brain. Remember my story back in Chapter 3? I played brain games with a deck of cards—memorizing the order of those cards. Soon, I graduated to more challenging mind exercises, such as learning facts and figures on flash cards. And I didn't stop there: I memorized all fifty states and their capitals, all the Oscar winners, the Scrabble dictionary, and then more than 80,000 zip codes. Be creative and engage your mind as you move your body.

Engage In Resistance Training (Working Out with Weights) Three Days a Week

▶ Do some light cardio workouts first, such as walking a half mile or so on an indoor track.

▶ Spend fifteen minutes stretching. Focus on these regions of your body: your back, legs, feet, ankles, shoulders, and arms. Go ahead and meditate as you stretch. The point is this: Strive to relax through proper stretching and breathing; make every effort to set your mind on peaceful thoughts.

▶ You can lift free weights (barbells) or make your way through circuit machines. I recommend the machines.

▶ Use proper form as you lift and use a full range of motion. In other words, don't arch your back, strain your neck, or rock your body to generate momentum. Not only can these maneuvers cause injury, but they also make the exercises less effective.

▶ Breathe as you execute each move. First, exhale through your mouth as you lift the weight and inhale deeply through your nose as you lower it. Breathing properly enables oxygen to reach your muscles.

▶ Work with a licensed gym trainer to help you customize the perfect routine for you.

Go for a Walk Five Days a Week

▶ When the weather is bad, use an indoor track at the gym or walk at the mall or at your office building.

▶ When the weather is good, get out and enjoy nature. Use all five senses and be aware of your surroundings.

▶ Use this time to socialize. Walk with your partner or with a friend.

▶ Try to walk for at least thirty minutes, which will rev up your metabolism. There are tons of studies that prove the single biggest benefit of taking a walk: It extends our lives.

MY WEEKLY EXERCISE
CHECKLIST

Choose two or three items from this list and incorporate them into your week.

☐ Take a 20-minute walk each evening around your neighborhood.

☐ Go for a Saturday-morning bike ride.

☐ Hit the weights at a gym three days a week.

☐ Engage in a once-a-week hike at a local park, the mountains, or the beach.

☐ Swim and do yoga at the YMCA (or other health club).

☐ Play brain games as you exercise on a stationary bike.

☐ Jog three nights a week at a local park or on an indoor track.

☐ Take a karate class with your partner.

☐ Get up early three days a week and stretch together.

☐ Pop an aerobic-style game in the Wii, Xbox, or PlayStation and work out together.

✓ **Health Trick #1:** Does it take you a long time to clear out the sleep fog when you wake up? If so, you may find that exercising in the morning before you start your day makes a big difference. In addition to clearing out the cobwebs, it also primes you for learning throughout the day.

✓ **Health Trick #2:** Physical activities that require hand-eye coordination or complex motor skills are particularly beneficial for brain building.

✓ **Health Trick #3:** Exercise breaks can help you get past mental fatigue and afternoon slumps. Even a short walk or a few jumping jacks can be enough to reboot your brain.

FUELING A HEALTHIER MIND WITH A HEALTHIER DIET

Consider what you are putting into your body, and strive to eat a healthy, balanced diet. The stresses of everyday life provoke some people to eat too little, others too much, or to eat unhealthy foods. Keep your health in mind when the pressures of life nudge you toward the fridge.

A well-balanced diet is crucial to good health, and it will enable you to improve your thinking. Certain foods and drinks can stimulate our bodies and actually trigger anxiety. In other words, that daily run to your favorite coffee spot is a fun vice, but in the long run it just might be taking a toll on your health: Think about the caffeine, sugar, and fat you're putting into your body. Think about how you feel after your body crashes. More stressed . . . right?

Here are some important dietary steps that I guarantee will reap profound benefits:

Cut Back on Caffeine. You're probably getting more of this than you think, especially if you consume daily doses of coffee, tea, chocolate, energy drinks, and soft drinks like Coke or Mountain Dew.

What happens inside our bodies: Caffeine stimulates the nervous system, which—as you know—triggers the release of adrenaline, making us feel nervous and jittery. Some medical professionals claim that there is a link between caffeine intake and high blood pressure, as well as high cholesterol levels.[45]

My advice: Consume caffeinated beverages in moderation. For example, no more than two cups of coffee in the morning. This will provide more than enough caffeine to increase your alertness and increase activity in your muscles, nervous system, and heart. But keep in mind that, in excess, caffeine can increase our stress levels.

Limit or Eliminate Alcohol. It's ironic really. Some people drink beer or wine to calm their nerves. But in reality, consuming large amounts of alcohol actually makes us feel more stressed-out.

What happens inside our bodies: Again, adrenaline is the culprit. Alcohol stimulates the secretion of this chemical, which affects the nervous tension. The result? When the buzz wears off, we end up feeling irritable, and we may even struggle to fall asleep. Excess alcohol can increase fat deposits in the heart, decrease the immune function, and limit the ability of the liver to remove toxins from the body.

My advice: Like caffeine, a glass or two of red wine with a meal can be a very useful drug and has even been shown to benefit the cardiovascular system. But use common sense: Alcohol is addictive and can be easily abused. Moderation is the key.

Reduce Your Sugar Intake. Our craving for sweets starts at an early age. Yet understand this: Sugar has no essential nutrients. It gives us a quick boost of energy, and then we crash.

What happens inside our bodies: Our adrenal glands become exhausted—i.e. the crash—and we begin feeling irritable and usually have difficulty concentrating. We may even feel a bit depressed.

In addition, consuming large quantities of sugar is bad for the pancreas, and it increases the possibility of developing diabetes.

My advice: Keep your blood sugar constant, and never use sugar as a "pick-me-up."

Use Salt Sparingly. In excess, salt (or sodium chloride) can increase our blood pressure. It's as plain and simple as that.

What happens inside our bodies: In excess, it depletes adrenal glands, and can cause emotional instability.

My advice: Use a salt substitute that has potassium rather than sodium. Avoid junk foods (such as potato chips) and foods cured with salt such as bacon and ham.

Cut Back on Fatty Foods. Avoid the consumption of foods rich in saturated fats. Fats cause obesity and put unnecessary stress on the cardiovascular system. High fat is believed to cause breast, colon and prostate cancers.

EAT THIS, NOT THAT . . .

Foods to Eat

- Whole grains promote the production of the brain neurotransmitter serotonin, which increases your sense of well-being.
- Green, yellow, and orange vegetables are all rich in minerals, vitamins, and phytochemicals, which boost immune response and protect against disease. Our brain's production of serotonin is sensitive to our diet. Eating more vegetables can increase our brain's serotonin production. This increase is due to improved absorption of the amino acid L-tryptophan. (Vegetables contain the natural, safe, form of L-tryptophan.) Meats contain natural L-tryptophan also, but when you eat meat, the L-tryptophan has to compete with so many other amino acids for absorption that it loses out. The net result is that you get better absorption of L-tryptophan when you eat vegetables.
- Eat more fiber. Stress results in cramps and constipation. Eat more fiber to keep your digestive system moving. Your meals should provide at least

25 grams of fiber per day. Fruits, vegetables, and grains are excellent sources of fiber. For breakfast, eat whole fruits instead of just juice, and whole-grain cereals and fiber-fortified muffins.

- Eat a meal high in carbohydrates. Carbohydrates trigger release of the brain neurotransmitter serotonin, which soothes you. Good sources of carbohydrates include rice, pasta, potatoes, breads, air-popped popcorn, and low-cal cookies. Experts suggest that the carbohydrates present in a baked potato or a cup of spaghetti or white rice are enough to relieve the anxiety of a stressful day.

Foods to Avoid

- Fried foods and foods rich in fat are very immune-depressing, especially when stress is doing that, as well.
- Eliminate bad trans fats. According to Daniel G. Amen, M.D., and other medical experts, these have no known health benefits and there's no safe level of consumption.
- Foods high in sugar.

Teas to Drink

Many natural teas are excellent options for relieving stress and anxiety, as well as for promoting digestive health. Here are three of my favorites:

Tea	Benefits	Precautions
Peppermint The menthol in peppermint leaves is a natural muscle relaxant.	• A natural tranquilizer, offering a relaxing effect • Promotes a sense of calm and well-being • Ideal at bedtime	Not recommended for pregnant women
Passionflower The flavone chrysin contained in passion flower has anti-anxiety benefits.	• Used for nerve-calming purposes • Relieves tension and relaxes muscles • Higher doses can be used to treat insomnia	Not recommended for pregnant women or children under six
Chamomile Chamomile is the go-to tea for reducing stress and anxiety, even for treating insomnia.	• Reduces irritability • Relieves nervous tension and relaxes muscles • Promotes sleep	Always use with caution Seek the advice of your physician first

ESSENTIAL STEPS TO REVVING UP ENERGY AND IMPROVING SELF-ESTEEM

☐ *Exercise*—weekly, if not daily. Without question, the chemicals produced during moderate exercise can enhance the function of the immune system, as well as train your body to deal with stress.

☐ *Breathe*—slowly to the count of six, and then breathe out slowly to the count of six. Do this for five minutes; gradually increase to 20 minutes over time. (More on this topic in Chapter 10.)

☐ *Eat*—a healthy, balanced diet. Stress and worrying provoke some people to skip meals or to eat too little, and others too much or unhealthy foods.

☐ *Drink*—an appropriate amount of water every day. It flushes toxins out of vital organs and carries nutrients to your cells. How much? That depends on your health, how active you are, and where you live.

☐ *Laugh*—it lifts your spirits, especially if you feel run-down. It's a good idea to avoid taking yourself too seriously and to laugh at your shortcomings.

☐ *Savor*—a moment with your partner, a walk in the park, a piece of art, a song, time spent outdoors, etc. What's more, getting sunshine and fresh air daily can be good for your emotions and your health.

☐ *Detox*—by avoiding or limiting substances such as caffeine, nicotine, and alcohol.

☐ *Sleep*—for at least seven to nine hours every day for adults and more for teens and kids. A lack of sleep can inhibit your productivity, trigger anxiety, and it can lead to serious health consequences.

GETTING MORE REST AND SLEEP

It's not healthy to push through the day feeling weary and worn-out. The fact is, too little shut-eye can drain our brain.

"Sleep is absolutely vital to your health and well-being," explains Don Colbert, M.D. "During sleep, you actually recharge your mind and body. It allows your body to recuperate and restore itself from exhaustion."[46]

In addition, Dr. Colbert says sleep enables our cells to regenerate and rejuvenate because our bodies secrete growth hormones that repair tissues and organs. Therefore, a lack of sleep can lead to serious health consequences and jeopardize our safety and the safety of individuals around you. For example, short sleep duration is linked with:

+ Increased risk of motor vehicle accidents
+ Increase in body mass index—a greater likelihood of obesity due to an increased appetite
+ Increased risk of diabetes and heart problems

+ Increased risk for psychiatric conditions, including depression and substance abuse
+ Decreased ability to pay attention, react to signals, or remember new information

"We have a cleaning system that almost stops when we are awake and starts when we sleep. It's almost like opening and closing a faucet—it's that dramatic," says Dr. Maiken Nedergaard, M.D., codirector of the Center for Translational Neuromedicine at the University of Rochester Medical Center.

"The brain has different functional states when asleep and when awake," Dr. Nedergaard adds. "In fact, the restorative nature of sleep appears to be the result of the active clearance of the by-products of neural activity that accumulate during wakefulness. . . . You can think of it like having a house party. You can either entertain guests or clean up the house, but you can't really do both at the same time."[47]

MY MEMORY MAGIC PLANNING CHART
Rev Up Energy and Self-Esteem

Day	Aerobic and Anaerobic Exercise	Dietary Plan	Sleep and Rest Log	My Health Goals
Sunday				
Monday				
Tuesday				
Wednesday				
Thursday				
Friday				
Saturday				

LET'S TAKE OUR MIND TO THE NEXT LEVEL

With a desire to treat our entire body—paying close attention to the mind-body-emotions connection—we move the discussion to another brain-boosting key: building strong social relationships. First we'll pinpoint hidden motives by observing and interpreting nonverbal behavior, and then by employing Emotional Intelligence.

MY MEMORY MAGIC PLAN: AT-A-GLANCE STEPS

Brain-Booster No. 2: Rev Up Energy and Self-Esteem

- Launch Aerobic and Anaerobic Exercise
- Fuel a Healthier Mind with a Healthier Diet
- Get More Rest and Sleep

8

Brain-Booster No. 3: Pinpoint Hidden Motives

Deciphering the "Tells" of Nonverbal Behavior

The suspense was agonizing.

Special Agent Janell gripped her .38 revolver, aimed it at the front door of the house and froze. Two other agents fanned out on each side of her, while another pair slipped around to the back of the house. A sixth agent hugged a wall and inched his way to the porch.

The FBI had learned this address was the hideout of a dangerous fugitive. Now they were moving in for the arrest.

"Come out with your hands up," yelled an agent. "The place is completely surrounded!"

Silence. Then, faint movement somewhere inside.

"This is the FBI. Give it up—NOW!"

Still more silence.

Janell took a deep breath and swallowed. She was prepared for the worst. This seasoned foreign counterintelligence agent had seen it all during her twenty-year career. Janell had fingerprinted plenty of fugitives, cracked down on countless kidnappers, investigated a bunch of bank robberies, and had wiped out a whirlwind of white-collar crime. She had even spent some time chasing spies—and was determined to catch this man too.

Janell was driven by a philosophy she had learned long ago, and it had always served her well: "Keep your eyes wide open, assume nothing . . . and read the nonverbals."

Suddenly, the lead agent reared back his leg and thrust it against the door with massive force. His foot connected with the weathered wood—then kept going. He punched a hole through the bottom half of the rickety door, then stood helpless. He was stuck.

What would happen next? Would bullets begin to fly? Would the FBI get their man—without losing one of their own?

Seconds later, a confused mother, cradling a baby in her arms, stuck out her head out a window. She looked at the hole in her door and gasped.

It appeared that the FBI had received a bad tip—and that their fugitive was nowhere in sight. Yet Janell wasn't about to put away her gun just yet, even though the scene looked like something from a cheesy reality cop show. Her partner yanked his foot out of the broken door and invited the young mother to step onto the porch. The woman took a seat on a metal patio chair, and the lead agent began questioning her. Janell tucked her gun in her holster and observed the exchange.

She noticed that the woman held her child close to her face, repeatedly kissing the baby on the head each time she answered a question. Her body seemed stiff, and her breathing was heavy. One hand rubbed her child's back in a consoling, pacifying manner, while her left foot tapped the floor. She was obviously nervous. Perhaps shaken up by all the commotion? Then again . . . maybe she was hiding something.

"Have you ever seen this man?" Janell's partner asked as he held up a photo of the fugitive.

At that very moment, the woman's feet seemed to freeze in place and for a split second her head started to nod "yes" as her mouth formed the words "NO! No . . . I've never seen that man before."

She kissed the baby again, and her eyes glanced briefly toward a storage unit near the side of the house. It was an oversized plastic container that probably held ceramic pots, hoses, and cushions . . . and was obviously large enough to hide a full-grown man.

Janell knew something wasn't quite right with this picture.

Her instincts had helped her monitor the activities of spies, report their activities, and stop them from gaining technology or selling important secrets to other countries. Her instincts were usually right.

This young lady wants to talk, but she's terrified, Janell thought to herself. *Her body language is pointing us to what's obvious: Our man is most definitely here.*

Janell caught her partner's eye and motioned toward the storage container. He knew exactly what she was thinking. As the lead agent distracted the woman, Janell and three other investigators aimed their weapons. A fourth one kicked open the lid of the container.

Two hands slowly rose toward the sky as a voice yelled, "Don't shoot! I surrender."

Janell smiled. Once again, keeping her eyes wide open, assuming nothing, and reading the nonverbals had paid off beautifully.

◆

Janell's ability to quickly read people and detect deception is a skill you and I can develop too. We can learn the secrets FBI agents know. We can decipher the tells of nonverbal behaviors and uncover the hidden emotions of those around us: friends, acquaintances, coworkers . . . and especially those we love deeply—husbands, wives, kids.

Imagine making the sale because you could practically read a customer's mind. Imagine responding to a loved one's needs without being asked—all because you could *see* that person's needs and *hear* their emotions. Cogmental Intelligence arms us with the essential knowledge we need to build better relationships as we sharpen our thinking, regain our mental edge . . . and improve our quality of life.

Strong social relationships stimulate the brain and nurture the psyche. In fact, connecting with others and relating to people on a deeper level improves mental health. In this chapter as well as the next, we'll mix Emotional Intelligence (EI) with deception detection techniques for a powerful way to read, relate to, and improve our connections with others. Warning: As we dive into our conversation, you'll begin feeling as if you've been sprayed with a fire hose! Learning what Janell and other FBI agents know is a fascinating pursuit with a wealth of details, which no doubt will seriously pay off in your life. As you get the hang of observing and accurately reading people, you'll begin to figure out how they make decisions and be able to predict their choices. And here's something else you'll find helpful: Since volumes have been written about deception detection, I'm arming you with just the fundamentals, and I'm sharing it through the lens of achieving better relationships so you can be a healthier, more fulfilled person—that holistic mind-body-emotions approach we've been talking about.

So, what are we getting into here? Basically, deception detection involves the examination of body language—nonverbal communication such as posture shifts, gaze aversion, and foot and hand movements. As I mentioned before, you'll gain the ability to recognize the unspoken subtext of a conversation.

Not only will I show you how to use concerted observation to decode verbal tells and nonverbal behavior, I'll help you tie these skills with the basics of EI. In Chapter 9 you'll meet Jordan and

Kristen, a young couple who are using these techniques to become more emotionally self-aware. Most important, they're learning how to communicate better and to experience more meaningful connections with each other and with others.

And that's the whole point of this chapter (as well as the next one). Unlocking the motives of others can lead to stronger interpersonal connections and greater influence—at home and at work. And better relationships, as I pointed out, can lead to a better brain.

I think it's time to get started. Ready or not, I'm aiming the fire hose!

READING BODY LANGUAGE

Even though our mouths can make a lot of noise—laughing, crying, cheering, and screaming—amazingly, it's not our voices or our words that speak the loudest. Instead, it's all those nonverbal signals our bodies communicate every second of every day: facial expressions, gestures, posture, tone of voice, and level of eye contact. A genuine smile that lights up the face can put someone at ease, build trust, and draw others toward us. On the other hand, a scowl, a pointing finger, or an aggressive stance can offend, confuse, and undermine what we're trying to convey.

Experts say much of our nonverbal signaling is automatic and performed outside our conscious awareness and control. Each one, right along with its physical expression, is an integral part of social interaction. They tell the world how we feel and, in turn, they affect how we are treated.[48] The gestures we make, the position in which we hold our bodies, the expressions we wear on our faces, and the nonverbal qualities of our speech all communicate volumes about ourselves and our state of mind.[49]

The trick is learning to decode these signals.

Let's explore how to speed-read people by understanding the basics of body language: What the face, arms, shoulders, torso, hands, and feet reveal about moods and motives.

Nonverbal Signals of the Face

More than sixty muscles covering the head and neck control the mouth, lips, eyes, nose, forehead, and jaw . . . enabling us to share more than ten thousand different expressions.[50] Our faces become relaxed when we're happy and tense when we're upset, instantly communicating our pleasure or displeasure. And each face—whether it's fresh and young or wise and timeworn—speaks a universal language that transcends cultures and countries. In fact, researchers have determined that there are universal facial expressions that signal seven different emotions: *anger, contempt, disgust, fear, joy, sadness,* and *surprise.*[51]

Here's what fascinates me most: Pioneer psychologist Paul Ekman, Ph.D., discovered micro expressions—short facial gestures every human makes when they feel an intense emotion. These expressions are so fast that if you blink you'll miss them, yet they are likely signs of concealed emotions.[52]

When it comes to reading body language, observing the face is a key to understanding someone's hidden emotions. Let's zero in on two important regions of the face—and what they may be communicating nonverbally.

Reading the Lips

Two of history's most intriguing lips belong to an iconic face: the mysterious Renaissance woman in the *Mona Lisa.* One minute she appears to be smiling, and then the next our brains play a trick on us—and the smile seems to fade. Is she amused or upset? Positive or skeptical? How did Leonardo da Vinci capture such an ambiguous expression? And what are those famous lips trying to communicate?

While that mystery may never be solved, here's something we do know: Smiling is one of the most powerful body language signals. At the same time, it's often misread.

For some, making the effort to flex forty-two muscles around the mouth may be a genuine display of warmth and happiness. But for others, a smile may be used to express sarcasm and cynicism— and even be used as a way to conceal true emotions. Human behavior expert David J. Lieberman, Ph.D., warns us to beware of the smile that doesn't seem happy. "Deception expressions are often confined to the mouth area," he says. "A smile that's genuine lights up the whole face. When a smile is forced, the person's mouth is closed and tight and there's no movement in the eyes or forehead."[53]

To me, the lips play a big role in reading body language. I notice everything from crinkling corners to pressing them together tightly—tells that usually mean something's up. For example, chewing on the bottom lip may indicate that the individual is experiencing feelings of worry, fear, or insecurity. Here are other signals I look for:

+ *Pursed lips.* Tightening the lips might be an indicator of distaste, disapproval, or distrust.
+ *Covering the mouth.* When people want to hide an emotional reaction, they might cover their mouths in order to avoid displaying smiles or smirks.
+ *Turned up or down.* Slight changes in the mouth can also be subtle indicators of what a person is feeling. When the mouth is slightly turned up, it might mean that the person is feeling happy or optimistic. On the other hand, a slightly down-turned mouth or even an outright grimace can be an indicator of sadness, disapproval.

Reading the Eyes

Just as our facial expressions speak a universal language, it's often said that our eyes are like windows into our souls. They reveal whether we're telling the truth or lying; whether we're kind or mean-spirited. So if someone covers their eyes, it's time to take notice. Psychologists say we can accurately decipher someone's emotions from their gaze. In fact, eye contact is the crucial first step for "resonance," a term psychologists use to describe a person's ability to read someone else's emotions.[54]

Research has shown that, when we like something we see, our pupils dilate; when we don't, they constrict. We have no conscious control over our pupils, and they respond to both external stimuli (for example, changes in light) and internal stimuli (such as thoughts) in fractions of a second.[55]

When a person looks directly into your eyes while having a conversation, it indicates that they are interested and paying attention. However, prolonged eye contact can feel threatening. On the other hand, breaking eye contact and frequently looking away might indicate that the person is distracted, uncomfortable, or trying to conceal his or her real feelings.

Nonverbal Signals of the Arms, Shoulders, and Torso

How we hold our bodies can also serve as an important part of body language. The term *posture* refers to how we hold our bodies as well as the overall physical form of an individual. Posture can convey a wealth of information about how a person is feeling as well as hints about personality characteristics, such as whether a person is confident, open, or submissive.

Sitting up straight, for example, may indicate that a person is focused and paying attention to what's going on. Sitting with the body hunched forward, on the other hand, can imply that the person is bored or indifferent.

When you are trying to read body language, try to notice some of the signals that a person's posture can send.

+ *Open posture.* Keeping the trunk of the body open and exposed indicates friendliness, openness, and willingness.
+ *Closed posture.* Hiding the trunk of the body, often by hunching forward and keeping the arms and legs crossed, can be an indicator of hostility, unfriendliness, and anxiety.
+ *Crossed arms.* This might indicate that a person feels defensive, self-protective, or closed-off.

Nonverbal Signals of the Hands

Observe the position of the hands, as well as hand gestures, and you'll uncover useful clues to what someone might be thinking. In fact, I run through a mental checklist when I meet someone for the first time. Are their hands clasped, in a steeple position, or in their pockets? And where are their thumbs? (Hidden or visible?) Next, I assess their handshake. Was it short, sweaty, and wimpy? Was it too firm, too dominant, and uncomfortably too long? Was it natural—solid, genuine, and lasting an appropriate length of time?

Why does any of this matter? Let's find out.

+ *Hands tucked in pockets.* This can mean that someone is feeling relaxed, comfortable, and casual or it can indicate nervousness . . . even outright deception. Distinguishing between the two depends upon some key factors: the setting (casual, at home . . . or formal, in the workplace), whether you know this individual, and the position of the person's head, shoulders, and torso. Are they hunched over or slouching (the turtle effect) or are they standing erect with their shoulders out (a sign of confidence)?

+ *Hands that hide thumbs.* Another giveaway is the location of the thumbs. Body language experts agree that tucking your thumbs in your pockets (with your fingers dangling out) signals low confidence, insecurity, and social discomfort. To the trained eye it communicates, "I don't feel good about myself." On the other hand (no pun intended), thumbs extending upward signals high confidence and positive thinking.

+ *Hands that tremble.* Unless the person has a neurological disorder, this is a pretty good clue that he or she is nervous, fearful, shaken-up, or traumatized. And what seems to be the opposite—frozen hands—could be an indication of lying. "Research tells us liars tend to gesture less, touch less, and move their arms and legs less than honest people," explains author and former FBI agent Joe Navarro.[56]

+ *Hands that are "steepling."* This looks a lot like a position of prayer: Hands in this position are spread out fingertip to fingertip and resemble the top of a church steeple. It's commonly believed that this gesture signals high confidence, instantly communicating self-assurance and competence.

+ *Hands with pointing fingers.* Unconscious pointing can also speak volumes. When making hand gestures, a person will point in the general direction of the person they share an affinity with (this nonverbal cue is especially important to watch for during meetings and when interacting in groups).

+ *Hands that support the chin.* Ever been in a deep conversation with someone and you notice them resting an elbow on a table with their hand tucked underneath their chin? This is a pretty good indication that they're really into what you have to say. Now if they support their head with both elbows on the table and their eyes seem glazed over . . . well, I think you get the picture. (Their body language is shouting, *I'm bored!*)

+ *Hands placed on the hips.* If I encountered someone in this stance, blocking my way on a Philadelphia street, I'd instantly perceive this as a sign of aggressiveness. But if that same person is a fellow speaker and I joined him or her on a stage in front of an audience, I'd tell myself, *Now that's confidence!* The context always matters.

+ *Hands that hold objects—such as notepads or clipboards.* Disregard what I'm about to say if the person you are interacting with is taking notes as you talk. (For example, if he or she is a journalist, a police officer, a therapist, a coach . . . you get the idea.) Otherwise, here's something to consider: Holding an object (such as a pad of paper) can serve as a barrier, and it can indicate that the person you are talking to feels vulnerable, nervous, or that they are hiding something.

+ *Rapidly tapping fingers or fidgeting.* This can be a sign that a person is bored, impatient, or frustrated.

Nonverbal Signals of the Feet

We started at the face and made our way down the body to a region that rarely ever lies: the feet. While most people focus on the eyes or person's overall stance, they overlook important clues that the legs and feet can tell us. What are they missing?

The first thing I look for is the direction of the feet. When standing or sitting, a person will generally point their feet in the direction they want to go. So if you notice that someone's feet are pointed in your direction, this can be a good indication that they have a favorable opinion of you. This applies to one-on-one interaction and group interaction. In fact, you can tell a lot about group dynamics just by studying the body language of people involved, particularly which way their feet are pointing.

If someone appears to be engaged in conversation with you, but their feet are pointing in the direction of someone else, it's likely he or she would rather talk to that person (regardless if the upper body cues suggest otherwise).

Here are some other signals to note:

+ *Crossed legs.* This indicates that a person is feeling closed off or in need of privacy.
+ *Tapping toes.* When a person is anxious (or just full of too much caffeine) their feet will twitch, tap, and move rapidly. But Joe Navarro points out that "happy feet" wiggle and bounce with joy, so it's important to discern carefully.
+ *Toes pointed up.* This usually indicates that a person is happy and calm.
+ *Interlocking ankles.* Sometimes individuals interlock their feet or wrap them around the legs of a chair when they feel insecure or threatened.
+ *Crossed legs while standing.* People who stand this way are usually quite calm and confident.

GETTING TO THE TRUTH

Deception detection is a fascinating study of body language that seeks to uncover reliable behavioral indicators of deception—and it, too, is a big part of my program. Those who master this skill end up possessing a powerful key to unlocking truth.

The key to mastering the art of deception detection is learning how to skillfully use all of your senses. Deceptive behavior can be identified within the first couple of seconds after a question is asked (verbal or nonverbal).

Focus, focus, focus!

Be a good listener. This is a great way to observe deceptive behavior and strengthen your intuitive sense. I like to get a baseline behavior by asking yes or no questions. The yes or no approach comes from several years of being a mentalist.

Step 1: Decipher Verbal Clues. After a question is asked, you listen for . . .

- a change in their voice tone
- a softening in their voice from the baseline
- stress in their voice
- no contractions
- vague answers
- hesitation

Step 2: Decipher Nonverbal Clues. After a question is asked, you watch for . . .

+ slight blushing
+ fidgeting (fingers, feet, etc.)
+ lip nibbling (Bill Clinton)
+ lip puckering
+ nose crinkling (It usually means they don't like something.)
+ changes in blink pattern changes after being asked a question (more or less frequent)
+ excessive eye-blinking
+ eyes looking briefly look away (even for just a split second)
+ dilated pupils (They may be excited or lying!)
+ noticeable swallowing
+ excessive yawning

Step 3: Decipher the Real Top Secret Stuff! From years of personal research as a mentalist! More things that can be observed:

+ a sense of imminent danger
+ threats (which trigger your flight response)
+ confidence/insecurity (hand to face or sudden nervous habits like fixing their tie, pulling on their shirt, twisting their hair or other grooming habits—definitely nervous or suspicious)
+ friendliness (or unfriendliness)
+ comfort/discomfort (revealed through pacifying behaviors)
+ confusion
+ key emotions, especially the big six: happiness, sadness, fear, disgust, surprise, anger. Strong emotions cloud our

perception of reality. Each emotional state is either self-induced, externally caused, or is a combination of the two. Anyone who uses any of these is attempting to move you from logic to emotion, in an attempt to manipulate you. In the process, the truth gets lost because you are not operating logically and cannot effectively see the evidence before you.[57]

My Memory Magic Exercise
Pinpoint Hidden Motives

Read Body Language

As you fill out this section, answer these three questions: *(1) What emotions am I uncovering through body language? (2) What hidden motives am I uncovering? (3) How can I step into other people's shoes and show empathy?*

Nonverbal Signals of the Face—Here's what I'm observing in some of my key relationships:
Family:

_____

_____

Friends:

_____

_____

Coworkers:

_____

_____

Nonverbal Signals of the Arms, Shoulders, and Torso—Here's what I'm observing in some of my key relationships:
Family:

_____

_____

Friends:

_____

_____

Coworkers:

_____

_____

Nonverbal Signals of the Hands—Here's what I'm observing in some of my key relationships:
Family:

_____

_____

Friends:

_____

_____

Coworkers:

_____

_____

Nonverbal Signals of the Feet—Here's what I'm observing in some of my key relationships:
Family:

_____

_____

Friends:

_____

_____

Coworkers:

_____

_____

Get to the Truth
Here's what I'm observing as I . . .

Decipher Verbal Clues

_____

_____

Decipher Nonverbal Clues

_____

_____

Decipher the Real Top Secret Stuff

_____

_____

LET'S TAKE OUR MINDS
TO THE NEXT LEVEL

When we take the time to observe others, we can't help but notice the unique ways in which people reveal their moods and emotions, not to mention their hidden motives. Tuning in to body language is a huge part of social awareness. In the next chapter, we'll take the people-watching skills we learned here and apply them to those we interact with. We'll discover that strong social relationships stimulate the brain and nurture the psyche. In fact, connecting with others and relating to people on a deeper level improves mental health.

MY MEMORY MAGIC PLAN:
AT-A-GLANCE STEPS

Brain-Booster No. 3: Pinpoint Hidden Motives

- Read Body Language
- Get to the Truth

9

Brain-Booster No. 4:
Build Better Relationships

The Keys to Unlocking Solid Connections

All evening Jordan had trouble talking to his fiancée, Kristen. Now he'd reached his breaking point. *What's with her? What does she want from me?*

It was a special night—Kristen's thirtieth birthday. Jordan had planned the perfect evening: a movie, dinner at the nicest restaurant in town . . . lots of conversation.

The place where they had come to dine was filled with the usual buzz of couples talking, clinking silverware, and mouthwatering aromas. But Jordan and Kristen sat at opposite ends of the table, Kristen toying with her chicken salad and Jordan munching his barbecued ribs as he replayed the evening in his mind.

I picked her up at her house and whisked her off to what I was sure would be a knockout evening. In the car, I told her all about my day at work and she—well, she didn't say a word. Then, when I opened the door to the restaurant and commented about how I love coming here with her, that's when she lobbed a stinging comment: "Are you sure you mean me, or one of your important clients at work?"

Jordan took a sip of water, then cleared his throat. *Got to diffuse this bomb.* "Uh, look—out the window. Isn't that the most beautiful night sky you've ever seen?"

"It's okay. But I saw lightning. It'll rain soon. It always does."

Okay, new approach. "Uh, are you having a bad day or something?"

Kristen just glared at him.

Jordan leaned back in his chair. "Please, talk to me. What's wrong? Why are you acting this way on your special night—your birthday?"

That's when she let him have it. "A few days ago, you called me. 'Hello, Kristen,' you said. 'Let's do something perfect for your birthday. I have some ideas.'"

"'Perfect,' I responded. 'Can't wait!'

"'Great,' you said. 'I'll work out the details, and then I'll call you.'

"I was thrilled, but you never called back . . . until, let's see, two hours ago. Then you said you'd pick me up around six and didn't show up until almost seven. And so I just sat there, feeling very foolish, wondering if you would even come at all. Then my mind began to play games with me: *What if he got in an accident? Is he okay? Maybe he isn't interested in me anymore. Maybe he forgot about my birthday. Does he think the world revolves around him . . . and that I'm supposed to just wait here by the phone? What an insensitive jerk!*"

Kristen moved forward and locked eyes with Jordan. "If you really care about me, then show some respect. Most of all . . . get a clue about what I'm thinking and feeling!"

Jordan just sat at the table with his mouth wide open—unsure about what to say.

BASIC CONNECTION NEEDS

Has this scenario touched a nerve? Have you been there too?

If two people don't connect very well, or if one person in the relationship feels hurt or unheard, problems arise, individuals grow apart . . . and the connection disintegrates. It's not rocket science, right? It happens all the time in the workplace and on the home front.

I'm sure you've noticed that the people we want to be closest to are, ironically, the ones who are sometimes deaf to the sound of your voice.

"I just can't read her sometimes!" one partner complains about the other. "What did I do wrong?"

"Why won't he listen to me?" someone fires back. "It's like he just doesn't hear me."

Here's something to think about, a fact I pointed out earlier: *The happiest people are those who are successful with relationships.* And research has proven that people who engage in social interaction display higher levels of cognitive performance than loners. In other words, positive social interaction is good for our brains—and ultimately improves our memory.

Yet most of us have experienced the emptiness that comes from feeling tuned out. That's because listening is an act of love—or, at a more basic level, an act of simple consideration. All communication requires two basic things: a sender and a receiver. (In other words, two people striving to connect.) This sounds pretty simple, but it's not. Most of us are very selective listeners, tuning in and out as our interests dictate. With all the extraneous noise and worthless static that bombards us daily, this skill can be a blessing. It is something else, however, when we find ourselves tuning out those we say we love.[58]

Yet this is exactly how Kristen felt: tuned out. And it hurt deeply because it came from the one person she wanted to connect with most.

Through the months, Kristen had invested her heart in this relationship—grounding it in friendship, trust, and honesty. Though Jordan's intentions were well meaning, it was important for the two of them to work through some communication static. Getting to know each other better and preparing for a life together depended upon it. But most important of all, learning three basic Cogmental Intelligence connection skills will not only strengthen their future marriage, it will enhance all of their interactions with others—on the home front and in the workplace. It begins with concerted observation and a listening heart.

A few days after expressing her frustration, Kristen took one more step—writing a note that detailed her deepest "connection needs." What this young lady shared applies to everyone:

Jordan, I need you to . . .

. . . not just see me, but hear me too.
. . . manage your own emotions so you can "hear" what's going on in my life.
. . . have empathy and respect for what I'm thinking and feeling.
. . . listen to me—with your ears and with your heart.
. . . consider, care, communicate.

Let's rewind the birthday dinner Jordan and Kristen experienced and learn what led up to that tense moment. Why did Kristen feel so tuned out? Why was Jordan so clueless about his fiancée's emotions? And in all fairness, what were some of the signals that Kristen completely missed? During the days and weeks before their eye-opening evening, the couple felt as if they'd been pummeled by a tsunami of stress—at work, with their siblings, and with each other.

Here's what happened.

✦

One week before Jordan's big celebration with his fiancée, he was called into his boss's office. As he took a seat at one end of the CEO's sprawling mahogany conference table, his heart began to pound right out of his chest. He knew he was in trouble.

"I'll get right to the point," the CEO barked. "You're a talented engineer, but lately your work has been sloppy."

His boss held up plans for a valve mold that Jordan had designed. Unfortunately, the dimensions were off, which resulted in a faulty product and a huge manufacturing blunder. "Do you know how much this mistake cost us?" the CEO asked.

Jordan just swallowed.

"More than I pay you in a year," his boss answered for him. "But I'm giving you another chance. Correct this, and you keep your job."

Jordan felt a mix of emotions—mostly relief. But it meant enduring a week from hell: long hours at his computer, no lunch breaks, late nights . . . and very little time with Kristen. That included the evening of his fiancée's birthday dinner.

Meanwhile, Kristen spent the week worrying about her younger brother. He was depressed and failing his last year of high school, which had sent Kristen's parents into a downward spiral of fear and shame.

"It's our fault," her mother insisted. "If we'd just been more involved in his life this wouldn't be happening. But I don't want to burden you with our troubles. You've got a wedding to plan!"

Kristen squeezed shut her eyes and chewed on her lower lip. *Yeah, right—a wedding!* she thought to herself. *As if I need more stress in my life. And is it still on? The one person I'm supposed to be closest to feels more like a stranger these days.*

By the time the special dinner had rolled around, Kristen and Jordan were both emotional wrecks. When the young man looked into his fiancée's eyes and said, "Please, talk to me. What's wrong?" . . . he had missed a number of signals all week that would have answered that question. No doubt about it, Jordan deeply loved Kristen. Yet he was emotionally tuned out. And the same could be said for Kristen. Her own difficult circumstances clouded her vision and caused her to be equally shut down.

Being aware of each other's feelings and reconnecting were crucial next steps for the couple—and it was essential for them to move forward with care, consideration, and honest communication.

Spoiler alert: This love story has a happy ending.

Jordan and Kristen soon discovered a powerful way to break through their connection barriers. By combining deception detection techniques with key components of Emotional Intelligence, they learned how to identify core feelings, manage them, and reduce conflict through meaningful communication. It's all part of my brain-boosting program—Cogmental Intelligence (CI).

In the remainder of this chapter, I'll show you how to use three CI Connection Keys to unlock better relationships. We'll build on what we've learned in the last chapter about deciphering body language and detecting deception. Our goal: Uncover accurate emotions in ourselves and in others, and use this awareness to manage our behaviors and improve our relationships.

CI CONNECTION KEY #1:
EXERCISE EMOTIONAL INTELLIGENCE

Consider, Care, Communicate

As Jordan struggled to survive one of the worst weeks of his life, his emotions went on autopilot. Since his mind was so preoccupied with one thing—saving his job—he tuned out everyone and everything. Stress and adrenaline sent him into a fight-or-flight mode.

Who could blame him . . . right? Kristen certainly didn't.

Remember the tough week she had to endure? Yet instead of going on autopilot herself or allowing bitterness to fester and pool, she chose to demonstrate Emotional Intelligence. Kristen took the steps to *consider* the moment (self-awareness), *care* about what was happening in that moment (empathy), and *communicate* with honestly and clarity (relationship management).

Emotional Intelligence is all about our ability to recognize and understand the wide range of feelings in ourselves and in others. We exercise it as we make an effort to accurately read how we and others feel at any particular moment—especially the way in which these emotions are affecting a situation. We then use this awareness to manage our behavior and nurture meaningful communication. Our goal is to find a positive solution.

Exercising Emotional Intelligence enables us to improve relationships.

→ **So our first connection key unlocks hidden emotions as we . . .**

CONSIDER What's Happening in the Present Moment

In other words, being tuned in to what's happening inside our mind and body and aware of what's happening around us. In that way, Emotional Intelligence is about concerted observation. (Remember our discussion in the last chapter about body language?) You notice your life with a little distance, instead of reacting emotionally.

Through Emotional Intelligence we can know ourselves reasonably well, control our own emotions, and show empathy with the feelings of others. This involves mindfulness (being aware and understanding ourselves and others), being in control of our own thoughts, emotions, and needs, using empathy—putting ourselves in others' shoes—and communicating effectively.

CARE Enough to Control Our Own Emotions, So We Can "Hear" What's Going On

Part of Emotional Intelligence is knowing what you are feeling as it happens. Being able to give the emotion you experience a name enables you to both register its impact (which engages your limbic system) and also trigger control through greater involvement of other parts of the brain (cognitive structures).

This balance of thought and emotion gives you more control of the feelings you experience by engaging different structures in the brain. Emotional Intelligence increases awareness and provides better control. It lets you know when your approach to dealing with others is getting skewed.

COMMUNICATE with the Goal of Shared Meaning.

Conversation #1—How It Could Be . . .

The Other Person: "I really hate this restaurant, and I don't see why you insist upon coming here. What is 'New York–style pizza,' and why do you like it so much?"

You: "I hear you; I crave this kind of pizza and you don't. But do you think you could order something else on the menu? And next time we can go to your favorite place."

The Other Person: "Yeah, I guess so. I'll order a salad or something. But when it's my turn to choose, we're heading to the sushi place across town!"

You: "Gross! I hate raw fish, but I'll do it. Thanks for coming here."

The Other Person: "No problem. That's what couples do, right? They compromise."

Conversation #2—How It Usually Is . . .

The Other Person: "I really hate this restaurant, and I don't see why you insist upon coming here. What is 'New York–style pizza,' and why do you like it so much?"

You: "You complain every time I even mention the word *pizza*. What's your problem? Look—I like this food, so get over it!"

The Other Person: "You never listen to me when I disagree with you about something. Why can't you see things my way? Why can't you stop being so selfish and think about me for a change?"

You: "Because it's always your way or the highway—and I'm tired of it."

The Other Person: "I'm starting to get tired of these arguments. Why can't we connect?"

✦

So, which conversation is more common with your friends and family—even those you work with? Let me guess—the second one! Too bad, because Conversation #1 isn't that far out of touch with reality. In fact, as we exercise the skills of Emotional Intelligence, we recognize that this can actually be the regular mode of conversation. EI is based on an important feature of relationships: "Behavior breeds behavior."[59] What we say and how we communicate contributes to others' reactions, so EI requires us to be mindful of the effect we have.[60]

It all begins with an important nine-letter word: LISTENING.

"My spouse just doesn't listen to me" is the anthem of many couples. Likewise, it's a complaint echoed by those in the workplace: "I can't get through to my boss—she just doesn't hear me."

Listening is how meaningful connection really begins. Instead of engaging in a verbal tug-of-war with people in your life, follow these essential steps:

Begin with passive listening (or silence). Give the other person a chance to speak their mind. "I'm just not getting anything out of the divisional updates every Monday morning. Since they're optional for mid-level managers, and since I'm so busy, I think I'll stop attending them."

Give acknowledgment responses. Don't just stand there with a blank expression on your face. Even when you're listening passively, it's a good idea to make sincere comments, such as "I see" or "Oh?" that emphasize that you are paying attention.

Offer a "door opener." This is a simple, nonjudgmental statement, such as, "How would you feel about attending them every other week? I'll assign another manager to take the other weeks." How-you-feel questions are less threatening to others, and they help spark communication.

Exercise active listening with a communication style called shared meaning. Here's how it works:

+ You're frustrated because your fiancé was late picking you up for dinner, and he didn't even bother to call you; he just showed up on your doorstep. So you approach him and say, "We need to talk about this. I'd like you to hear my side."
+ Once you have his attention, you explain your point of view (which you've thought through ahead of time) without being interrupted.
+ Next, your fiancé repeats what he heard you say.
+ You then clarify or confirm what he said, ensuring that your thoughts and feelings have been heard accurately.
+ The process continues with him sharing his point of view, and you listening and repeating what he said.

The goal of shared meaning is to be heard accurately. And once you've had a chance to state your case and listen to that of another person, the foundation is set for communication—and for a fair solution to the problem at hand. A solution that's grounded on listening and being heard . . . not just another pointless conflict.

CI CONNECTION KEY #2:
TUNE IN VERBAL AND NONVERBAL SIGNALS

Read Body Language, Recognize the Unspoken Subtext of a Conversation, and Nurture the Ability to See and Hear Emotion

In Chapter 8 we explored the secrets FBI agents know. We learned how to decipher the tells of nonverbal behaviors and uncover the hidden emotions of those around us. Now it's time to apply these skills to our relationships on the home front and in the workplace. As Jordan and Kristen discovered, the signals are often there well before two people end up in a conflict. If we take the time to observe others and listen to them, we'll clue in to what they are really feeling and can plan an appropriate response. To get a complete read from a person, we must do a head-to-toe body language assessment.[61]

Tuning in verbal and nonverbal signals enables us to manage these signals.

→ **So our second connection key unlocks hidden emotions as we . . .**

Read Body Language

+ *Facial expressions:* When Jordan realized that having a "business-as-usual" conversation with his fiancée simply wasn't going to happen, his first response was a thoughtless question: *What's with her . . . what does she want from me?* Once he had taken a moment to tune in, he realized Kristen's facial expressions had signaled her true emotions—which she had been signaling all week long. For days leading up to their conflict, she had glared at him with scowls and frowns instead of the usual warmth and joy. Again, it doesn't take rocket science to clue in to these emotional tells—just thoughtful observation.

+ *Level of eye contact:* At first, Kristen had missed some key body language as well—especially when it came to reading her fiancé's eyes. Whenever Kristen would catch Jordan's gaze, his whole face would light up. That was the norm. But lately, and most certainly during Kristen's birthday dinner, Jordan's eyes seemed lost and sad. And even though he would attempt to smile, she knew that expression was masking other emotions. Not knowing what was going on with her fiancé, and feeling overwhelmed by her own stress, sent Kristen's brain reeling with all kinds of catastrophic thoughts: *Has Jordan lost interest in me? Is our relationship in trouble? Did I do something to hurt him?*

+ *Gestures and body posture:* It didn't take a body language expert to observe the stress in Jordan's and Kristen's life. As the couple sat at opposite ends of the dinner table, both their bodies were slouching with their shoulders rising toward their ears. It's commonly known as the turtle effect and is sometimes displayed by someone who feels unconfident, insecure, and highly uncomfortable. In this case, a couple that had been pummeled by that stress tsunami. Jordan was constantly massaging his neck (a pacifying behavior), while Kristen's arms seemed to be frozen at her sides.

+ *The hands and the feet:* All evening, Kristen noticed that Jordan was fidgety. When his hands weren't massaging his neck, his fingers were constantly tapping—right along with his feet. But every few seconds, it appeared that Jordan's hands were trembling—a pretty good clue that he was nervous or shaken-up about something. *This is weird,* Kristen thought, *and I can't sweep aside all the signals I've observed. Obviously something's up with him.* The frantic bride-to-be only assumed the worse.

Recognize the Unspoken Subtext of a Conversation

While our bodies are like billboards, communicating reliable nonverbal clues about our true emotions, it's equally important to pick up on verbal signals: tone, pitch, volume, and *how* something is said.

All week—and leading up to the moment when everything

came to a head during the stressful birthday dinner—Kristen could sense a change in Jordan's voice. It wasn't calm and playful, the way he had normally communicated. Instead, his words were hesitant, choppy, and concise. Jordan seemed preoccupied, which (as she later learned) was exactly the case!

As you consider your own significant relationships, what should you listen for in someone's voice? And how should you assess the important conversations at home or in the workplace? Here are three essential verbal categories I try to decode:

The Tone, Pitch, and Volume of Someone's Voice

I also consider things like clarity, cadence, context, and breathing as I tune in to verbal signals. Of course, several factors must be considered first, such as how well you know the person, as well as the setting of the conversation (home versus work, for example). Once I figure out a baseline for verbal communication, I ask myself two questions:

- *Is their tone confident and self-assured or hesitant and shaky?* Just as the wrong tone of someone's voice can instigate hurt feelings, or even an argument, the right tone can reveal warmth, trust, and a sense of humor. Decoding tone can unlock anger, deception, distrust, and fear.
- *What do their pitch, pacing, and volume reveal?* Is their voice nervous and choppy—filled with a lot of "ums" and "ahs"? Does their voice go up in tone or down in tone at the end of a sentence? For example, a down tone displays confidence and authority.

How Verbal Communication Is Delivered

Decoding verbal signals means going beyond *what* someone has to say and assessing *how* something is communicated. It's about the language we use, the way we construct sentences, the sound of our words and the personality we communicate. As we've discussed in this chapter, nonverbal communication consists of facial expressions, tone, cues, gestures, and pitch. So how is someone's tone delivered? Consider their style as you decode their signals.

+ *Humorous/Serious.* Communication is usually humorous and playful with those we have a connection with; serious with acquaintances, business associates and those in authority. So what does it mean if someone who is typically warm and playful suddenly shares something with a serious tone? In this case, tone captures my attention. What's going on in their life? Is there a hidden message here?
+ *Formal/Casual.* Bosses, experts, and business professionals usually communicate with a more formal tone and style.
+ *Respectful/Irreverent.* If someone you're in authority over (or someone you barely know) speaks to you with irreverence, it's time to dig in and take note. What's underneath the tone? What are they really trying to communicate?
+ *Enthusiastic/Monotone.* I also take note when someone who is typically enthusiastic becomes subdued and monotone in speech. This is a clear signal of a deeper emotion.

Nurture the Ability to See and Hear Emotion

Gathering accurate *nonverbal intelligence* takes a bit of detective work, which isn't easy. Yet knowing what to look for gives you the edge. Now you have the knowledge to break through the façades coworkers hide behind at work. Now you can protect yourself from lies, spin, and manipulation. And at home, you're ready to uncover honest emotion so you can achieve authentic connections with the ones you love. But before you make yourself a SPECIAL AGENT OF SECRET EMOTIONS badge, there's one more thing we need to learn: how to nurture the ability to see and hear emotion . . . *in a practical way.* In other words, we want all this emotional detective work to become second nature—otherwise it's pointless, right?

As I said in the last chapter, reading people takes *focus, focus, focus!* Becoming good at it requires *practice, practice, practice!* This is where CI Connection Key #1 really kicks in.

Become self-aware and clue in to your emotions first. The more open we are to our own emotions, the more easily we will be attuned to the emotions and feelings of others. So ask yourself this: *How do I feel?* Listen for feelings; let them just pop up. For example, *I feel tired. I feel anxious. I feel happy. I feel sad.* Refrain from judgment or comments, just like when you're listening to a child. If you hear a feeling you don't understand, or need more information about, ask some questions. For example, let's say you hear *I feel anxious.* Ask: *What am I anxious about?*

Once you discover the underlying reason for the anxiety, express empathy—do not judge. Let your Emotional Self know that you are going to figure out ways together to alleviate the anxiety. By tuning in your emotions, asking yourself questions, and accepting your feelings, your ability to guide your Emotional Self from a place of compassion and wisdom will develop.

Now it's time to look outward. Go ahead and observe the body language of others—each of the things we discussed the last two chapters. Watch for facial expressions, hand motions, gestures, and tone of voice.

Be in tune to someone's emotional truth. It's more important *how* a person says something than what they say. Studies have shown that 90 percent of the messages we receive from other people are nonverbal.

Be a good listener. To be empathetic, you have to really hear what the other person is telling you. To develop empathy, it's important to have all the details. Give the other person a chance to express themselves and refrain from interrupting.

Questions for Greater Self-Awareness:

→ *What's the source of my emotions?*
→ *What are some of my nonverbal tells that give away my feelings?*
→ *How do I behave when I'm under stress?*

Questions as I Observe Others:

→ *Is this expression or posture out of character?*
→ *Am I aware of anything going on that would cause this behavior?*
→ *Are my own emotions skewing my reaction to this behavior?*

Questions as I Manage My Relationships:

→ *How do my emotions affect others?*
→ *How do the emotions of others affect me?*
→ *Who and what pushes my buttons?*

CI CONNECTION KEY #3: IDENTIFY AND MANAGE FIVE BASIC EMOTIONS

Happiness, Sadness, Anger, Fear, and Shame

Human emotions have been researched, dissected, and debated ever since the birth of psychology—way back in 1879. But in modern times, famed psychologist Dr. Paul Ekman boiled it down to six basic states: *anger, disgust, fear, happiness, sadness,* and *surprise.* Ever since making that assertion, countless other experts have jumped on board, agreeing that these core emotions are building blocks of more complex feelings. *Excitement,* for example, could be a combination of fear and happiness. Just recently, however, a group of smart folks at the University of California–Berkeley, have pushed back, claiming that Dr. Ekman's list is too simplistic. They expanded his original six to twenty-seven distinct types of emotion. Here's a selection they've included on their list: *awe, awkwardness, calmness, confusion, horror, nostalgia, sexual desire, sympathy,* and *triumph.*[62]

Interesting, right? Yet before you add your own word to the list— like *overwhelmed*—let me tell you where I stand (and what has helped me). I lean toward yet another camp: The findings of Travis Bradberry and Jean Greaves, Ph.D.s, proponents of Emotional Intelligence (EI). They're more in tune with Dr. Ekman and have identified five basic emotions: *happiness, sadness, anger, fear,* and *shame.*

So why does any of this matter? As Drs. Bradberry and Greaves have observed, our brains are wired to make us emotional creatures, so our first reaction to an event is always going to be an emotional one. "But too often, we lack the skills to manage our emotions in the heat of the challenging problems that we face," they explain. "Good decisions require far more than factual knowledge. They are made using self-knowledge and emotional mastery when they're needed most."[63]

Navigating emotions isn't easy, and most of us aren't very good at recognizing the ones we're experiencing, let alone the feelings of others. The result: constant misunderstandings and missteps—and not just at home and with our loved ones. Think about a typical day in the workplace. A big part of management, leadership, human resources, and sales is being able to understand what people are really feeling. It's amazing when you consider that a single concession or action could avert so much conflict and wasted time, effort, and resources.[64]

Identifying and understanding emotions enables us to manage them.

→ **So our third connection key unlocks hidden emotions as we . . .**

Identify and manage five basic feelings. These are the emotions we experience as a result of our reactions to an event or a situation. Let's think of the following categories as the basic ingredients that get mixed up and baked into a much more complex emotional soufflé! Refer to the "Building Blocks of Emotion" chart on page 170 as you take a moment to explore each emotion in yourself and in others.

♦ *Happiness.* It isn't hard to miss in ourselves and in others. Most of us are drawn to happy people, and others are drawn to us when we express this emotion. It's an attractive mix of joy, cheerfulness, peace, and positive feelings . . . and has been said to relate to life satisfaction, gratefulness, and moments of pleasure.

→ **How I Feel:**
What makes me happy? (Share what's underneath these feelings.)

_____

_____

When I'm happy and positive, some of the emotions I feel are:

_____

_____

(For example: excited, fired up, gratified, contented.)

→ **Managing My Feelings:**
Here's what's actually going on inside me at this moment:

_____

_____

When I'm happy and positive, here's how I treat others:

_____

_____

→ **Observing Others:**
Here's what I observe in others when they're happy:

_____

_____

→ **Managing My Relationships:**
Here's how I can see the other person's perspective, tune in to their feelings, and have more empathy for them:

_____

_____

✦ *Sadness.* We try to avoid it like the plague, don't we? A kid cries, and we hand him an ice-cream cone. When adult friends seem hurt, let down, and disappointed, we do all we can to cheer them up. Yet sadness is a fact of life.

→ **How I Feel:**
What makes me sad? (Share what's underneath these feelings.)

_____

_____

When I'm sad and pessimistic or negative, some of the emotions I feel are:

_____

_____

(For example: alone, hurt, let down, upset)

→ **Managing My Feelings:**
Here's what's actually going on inside me at this moment:

_____

_____

When I'm sad and down, here's how I treat others:

_____

_____

→ **Observing Others:**
Here's what I observe in others when they're sad:

_____

_____

→ **Managing My Relationships:**
Here's how I can see the other person's perspective, tune in to their feelings, and have more empathy for them:

_____

_____

◆ *Anger.* We all feel it from time to time, and like sadness, it's a fact of life. Yet it's usually an unwanted emotion, and it makes us uncomfortable. (Some folks go out of their way to avoid it.) Low levels of anger can be triggered when we feel tired or stressed, and are described as "annoyed," "irritated," and "resistant." On the other hand, high levels can affect our ability to communicate, cause us to say or do hurtful things, and can make others feel threatened.

→ **How I Feel:**

What makes me angry? (Share what's underneath these feelings.)

_____

_____

When I'm angry, some of the emotions I feel are:

_____

_____

(For example: furious, betrayed, frustrated, touchy)

→ **Managing My Feelings:**

Here's what's actually going on inside me at this moment:

_____

_____

When I'm angry, here's how I treat others:

_____

_____

→ **Observing Others:**

Here's what I observe in others when they are angry:

_____

_____

→ **Managing My Relationships:**

Here's how I can see the other person's perspective, tune in to their feelings, and have more empathy for them:

_____

_____

◆ *Fear.* According to experts, this is an emotional response induced by a perceived threat, which causes a change in our brain and organ function, as well as in our behavior.[65] It can trigger the fight-or-flight response, leading us to stand our ground and strike back or to run away. High levels are described as "terrified" or "horrified," while low levels are labeled as "nervous" or "anxious."

→ **How I Feel:**

What makes me afraid? (Share what's underneath these feelings.)

_____

_____

When I'm fearful, some of the emotions I feel are:

_____

_____

(For example: petrified, shocked, threatened, unsure)

→ **Managing My Feelings:**

Here's what's actually going on inside me at this moment:

_____

_____

When I'm afraid, here's how I treat others:

_____

_____

→ **Observing Others:**

Here's what I observe in others when they're afraid:

_____

_____

→ **Managing My Relationships:**

Here's how I can see the other person's perspective, tune in to their feelings, and have more empathy for them:

_____

_____

✦ *Shame:* This is a powerful emotion that all too often holds people back, sending them into toxic, downward spirals. It's different from guilt, which is that pang we feel inside when we feel judged or when we've done something wrong. Shame, on the other hand, bubbles and pools inside and eats away at our core. It's how some people define themselves: They feel deeply flawed and even believe that their whole self is wrong . . . even irredeemable.

→ **How I Feel:**

What makes me ashamed? (Share what's underneath these feelings.)

_____

_____

When I'm ashamed, some of the emotions I feel are:

_____

_____

(For example: sorrowful, worthless, unworthy, regretful)

→ **Managing My Feelings:**

Here's what's actually going on inside me at this moment:

_____

_____

When I'm ashamed, here's how I treat others:

_____

_____

→ **Observing Others:**

Here's what I observe in others when they're ashamed:

_____

_____

→ **Managing My Relationships:**

Here's how I can see the other person's perspective, tune in to their feelings, and have more empathy for them:

_____

_____

BUILDING BLOCKS OF EMOTION

Level Of Emotion	Happy	Sad	Angry	Afraid	Ashamed
MILD	Calm	Disappointed	Annoyed	Anxious	Awkward
	Glad	Dissatisfied	Cranky	Nervous	Regretful
	Hopeful	Low	Critical	Suspicious	Ridiculous
	Peaceful	Moody	Displeased	Wary	Speechless
	Upbeat	Upset	Irritated	Worried	Silly
MODERATE	Cheerful	Distressed	Aggravated	Alarmed	Ashamed
	Delighted	Grieving	Disgusted	Apprehensive	Contrite
	Joyful	Heavy	Frustrated	Insecure	Embarrassed
	Relieved	Let-Down	Inflamed	Intimidated	Guilty
	Satisfied	Weepy	Mad	Threatened	Secretive
SEVERE	Elated	Anguished	Bitter	Horrified	Demeaned
	Excited	Depressed	Furious	Panicked	Disgraced
	Jubilant	Despairing	Irate	Petrified	Mortified
	Overjoyed	Hopeless	Livid	Shocked	Remorseful
	Thrilled	Miserable	Outraged	Terrorized	Worthless

PUTTING IT ALL TOGETHER

Since a key to achieving the mental edge is socialization, nothing is better for our minds (and our memories) than strong social relationships. And as we've learned in this book, nothing is better for improving relationships than learning how to read people. Those who master my Cogmental Intelligence (CI) skills end up possessing a powerful key to unlocking emotional truth and good mental health. It isn't hard to spot people who have clued in to my CI plan. These folks are (1) positive and happy, (2) they don't dwell on the past, (3) they know how to enjoy the moment and deal with disappointments, and (4) they strive to empathize with others.

MY MEMORY MAGIC EXERCISE

Build Better Relationships

Exercise Emotional Intelligence

As you fill out this section, refer back to your notes in CI Connection Key #3.

Consider the moment (self-awareness)—As I slow down, look inward, and strive to learn more about my true self, here's what I'm discovering:

_____

_____

Care about what is happening in that moment (empathy)—Here's what I'm observing in some of my key relationships:

Family:

_____

_____

Friends:

_____

_____

Coworkers:

_____

_____

Communicate with honestly and clarity (relationship management)—Here's how communicating with the goal of *shared meaning* is helping me manage key relationships:

Family:

_____

_____

Friends:

_____

_____

Coworkers:

_____

_____

Tune In Verbal and Nonverbal Signals

Here's what I'm observing as I . . .

Read Body Language

_____

_____

Recognize the Unspoken Subtext of a Conversation

_____

_____

Nurture the Ability to See and Hear Emotion

_____

_____

Identify and Manage Five Basic Emotions

Creating your own emotional vocabulary list can help you to better understand and manage your emotions. Using the "Building Blocks of Emotion" chart on page 170 as a starting point, expand your emotional vocabulary.

My Emotional Vocabulary List

Happiness:	Sadness:	Anger:	Fear:	Shame:

LET'S TAKE OUR MINDS TO THE NEXT LEVEL

Improving relationships is one piece of our brain-boosting puzzle. Here's a final one that ties together the various element of Cogmental Intelligence: increasing creativity and intuition.

CONNECT WITH CONVERSATION

MY MEMORY MAGIC PLAN: AT-A-GLANCE STEPS

Brain-Booster No. 4: Build Better Relationships

✦ Exercise Emotional Intelligence: *Consider, Care, Communicate*
✦ Tune In to Verbal and Nonverbal Signals: *Read Body Language, Recognize the Unspoken Subtext of a Conversation, and Nurture the Ability to See and Hear Emotion*
✦ Identify and Manage Five Basic Emotions: *Happiness, Sadness, Anger, Fear, and Shame*

Connecting with another person can be tricky . . . to say the least. It involves exercising our skills as a "good conversationalist." It requires us to take risks and to become vulnerable. It often means creating a conversation out of thin air. But I can't emphasize enough how important all this is. As we look someone in the eye and ask good questions, it makes them feel that we are truly interested in them as a person. This works with men and women alike . . . kids, adults, employers, checkout clerks at the store, and even our bosses. It's an art form that we develop over time.

One really good way to make a great impression conversationally is to ask questions. The typical "What do you like to do?" "What are your favorite meals?" "What did you think about the HR meeting this morning?" or "How 'bout them Cardinals (or pick your sports team)?" is never a bad place to start. Ask about hobbies, travels, family, or favorite movies, etc. Or talk about something you like and see if they catch interest.

It's important to be able to show interest in someone else's life, learning their interests and what gives them joy, as well as sharing in their hurts and challenges. It is a very appealing trait that opens the door to more conversations . . . and a deeper connection.

Get a clue about communication differences. For some people, a conversation is often a way to define a problem, debate the rights and wrongs, and find a solution. But others would rather have a friendly ear instead of advice. If at all possible, clue in to the communication styles of those you're trying to connect with. (Obviously, this will be easier with those you are close to; much harder with acquaintances.) For example, I have friends who are extroverts who view a conversation as a way of sharing their emotions with the listener. They talk until they feel better. On the other hand, I've met introverts who actually run out of words and shut down. (They simply don't know what else to talk about.) Understanding communication styles and differences will enable you to connect better with friends, family, and coworkers.

Make sure he/she has been heard. In addition to being heard, every person needs to be understood. So don't just nod your head a few times and think you're doing someone a favor. Hear the other person's heart. Engage in the conversation and show that you really care what the other person is thinking and feeling.

Connect with encouraging words. Mark Twain once said he could go for two months on a good compliment. Likewise, every one of us needs to be appreciated—to be applauded—for the awesome and unique person we are. We need others to recognize our strengths or sometimes just to prop us up in the places where we tend to lean a little. Honest compliments are simple and cost nothing to give, but we must not underestimate their worth.

10

Brain-Booster No. 5: Increase Creativity and Intuition

Clearing Away Negativity with Memitation Techniques

Connie loved her teenage daughter's contagious excitement—her animated gestures, her fall-on-the-floor giggle attacks, her goofy tales of a day in the life of a modern-day middle-schooler. The contented mom sat back and listened with amusement. Yet right in the middle of her child's story—PING! A stressful thought raced through Connie's mind: It was an image of her daughter being hurt in some way.

What if something bad happens to her at school?

PING! Another irrational fear swirled through the forty-nine-year-old's brain: It was the sinking feeling that she wasn't doing enough to protect and nurture her child.

Where are these thoughts coming from? Connie wondered. *I can't let them derail a joyful moment.*

Connie took a deep breath and swallowed, nodding her head every now and then—signaling that she was following the conversation. But internally she was trying to shake off the negativity.

The same frightening scenarios replayed over and over . . . and just wouldn't go away.

Connie took another deep breath and looked down for a second: *These are irrational thoughts,* she told herself. *They are not real; they don't have power over me.*

The ugly scenarios left Connie's mind after some proper breathing and a mental script that had helped her overcome stress in the past. She then reengaged with her daughter's story. Yet the weary mom was left with a knot in the pit of her stomach. *I've got to change my thinking.*

✦

Allison, thirty-five, had a tendency to get stuck on certain fears, locked into them, rethinking the same negative thought over and over. Even as a child her family labeled her a worrier: "You're obsessing again, Ali," her mom would tell her. "Just let it go and stop worrying so much."

Allison couldn't then—and she still couldn't now. This wife and mother of three got so worked up about stress, both real and imagined, that she found herself in the grip of a full-blown panic attack . . . as often as two or three times a month. They'd come out of the blue and usually involved irrational fears: *Is something bad going to happen to my kids? Is my husband okay? Does he still love me?*

Her heart raced, breathing turned to gasping, and she usually felt tightness in her chest. While the physical reactions peaked within a few minutes, the repetitive negative thoughts stuck around, constantly circling through her mind. And the more she tried to control them, the more powerful they became.

Maybe I'm just going crazy. I simply can't live this way. Something has to give.

Change Your Thinking, Improve Your Life

In order to improve our brains, and ultimately our lives, we must change the way we think. In this chapter, I'll show you how to clear away negativity with what I call Memitation techniques.

Here's the idea behind Memitation: Anxiety, stress, and worry can block our thinking and take a toll on our health. Stress is a big factor in forgetfulness, lack of focus, and an inability to concentrate. So gradually eliminating negative emotions and thoughts not only enhances emotional intelligence, it is the single most important thing that we can do for our brain. Therefore, I developed Memitation—my own unique mental exercise that mixes meditation with memorization. I define it this way: *The act of reviewing memorized information in quiet thought, while focusing on breathing.*

Breathing slowly and deeply is an important part of this activity. I begin by concentrating on the air flowing in and out for about three minutes, and then I focus on a positive experience in my life. This not only relaxes me, but it also reduces stress by lowering cortisol levels. Memitation also triggers the release of adenosine, a neurotransmitter that makes us tired and promotes sleep.

We'll wrap up the chapter with an exciting look at ways we can learn to think more creatively and boundlessly, to see the world the way the world's greatest minds have seen it. History's great minds knew how to think outside the box: to think creatively and limitlessly in order to harness their minds' power. They had an intuitive understanding of *how* to learn.

Let's begin by facing a deadly duo: stress and its killer cousin, negativity.

CLEARING AWAY STRESS AND NEGATIVITY

Our brain is part chemical factory, part German autobahn.

Information is transmitted from one nerve cell to the next by neurotransmitters. These chemical messengers race through the nerves, giving orders, "Full alert—get moving," or "Be calm and slow down!" They tell the brain to be happy, sad, anxious, or tranquil. They warn of emergencies and tell us when it's safe to rest.

How?

Stress Hormones are Pumped into the Bloodstream.

Each nerve cell (or neuron) releases small amounts of neurotransmitters, some of which trigger a reaction in the next neuron and some of which are reabsorbed by the original neuron (in a process known as reuptake).[66] The effects of this process on our bodies depend on lots of things: the type of neurotransmitter released, the amount that is produced or reabsorbed, the sensitivity of the receptors on the receiving neuron, and the location in the brain where the process is occurring.[67]

Excessive worrying and anxiety, however, cause the body's sympathetic nervous system to release large amounts of cortisol. These hormones can boost blood sugar levels and triglycerides (blood fats) that can be used by the body for fuel. "Cortisol is kind of like the after-burner," Eric T. Scalise, Ph.D., LPC, LMFT explains. "It gives everything a good kick. But too much can be a problem."

GABA

+ Chief inhibitory neurotransmitter in the central nervous system

+ Regulates neuronal excitability and helps us to calm down
+ Includes brain chemicals such as serotonin, dopamine, nor-adrenaline

Cortisol

+ Partners with adrenaline
+ Released in response to stress
+ Depletes GABA

Adrenaline Triggers the Fight-or-Flight Reaction.

Every time adrenaline is released in the body, the brain signals the blood supply to go to our major muscle groups—primarily our legs, our quads, and our largest muscle groups. Why? It's trying to help us determine if we should engage or disengage from a given situation. In other words, should we fight for our lives or head for the hills? But as blood is pumped to our muscles, guess where it isn't going? Our brains. Messages are being steered away from the thinking portion of the brain to the feeling part. That's why a stressful situation often sparks a wide range of emotions: fear, panic, anger, distrust, insecurity.

We go from "high alert" to "system crash."

When our adrenaline hormones are exhausted from overuse, our bodies crash and adrenaline is then under-produced in an attempt to recover from its overproduction. With an under-production of adrenaline during those crashing times, we will feel so vulnerable that even the smallest stressor can seem overwhelming. How each of these systems interacts with the other is profoundly influenced by our coping style and our psychological state.

When the GABA and cortisol hormones are in balance, we

usually feel pretty good—peaceful and in a happy, tranquil mood. But when the sad messengers outnumber the happy ones, we end up depressed, panicked, worried, and anxious.

"I am truly amazed by this process," Dr. Hart says. "Proper communication between our brain cells is all wonderfully complex and vitally essential to our sanity. Normal human emotions are determined by whether these neurotransmitters are successful in communicating their messages to your brain cells. On a typical day in the life of your brain, literally trillions of messages are sent and received by these neurotransmitters."[68]

Negative Effects of Stress

+ Stress damages almost every kind of cognition that exists.
+ It definitely damages memory.
+ It can hurt your motor skills.
+ When you are stressed out over a long period of time, it can eventually disrupt your immune response.
+ Stress can make you sicker more often.
+ It disrupts your ability to sleep.
+ Stress can make you depressed.
+ Stress can lower *all-around* performance!

Stress Symptoms

+ Stiff or tense muscles, especially in the neck and shoulders
+ Headaches
+ Sleep problems
+ Shakiness or tremors
+ Loss of interest in sex

- Weight loss or gain
- Restlessness
- Grinding teeth
- Difficulty completing work assignments
- Changes in the amount of alcohol or food you consume
- Taking up smoking
- Increased desire to be with or withdraw from others
- Overwhelming sense of tension
- Trouble relaxing
- Nervousness
- Quick temper
- Depression
- Poor concentration
- Trouble remembering things
- Loss of sense of humor

✓ **Stress-Buster Trick #1:** Oxytocin is one of the many neurotransmitter chemicals in our brain. It's known as the "love molecule" and is a great stress reducer! How can we activate this chemical? Here are three of my favorite ways: (1) Research shows that petting your dog can boost oxytocin levels in both you and your dog. (2) Yoga, meditation, and memitation are also connected with increasing oxytocin levels. (3) Playing card games like poker helps to relieve stress.

Out of Tune and Anxious

Ready to slow down, savor life, and get your world back in balance?

Take a look at what writer Tim Kreider published in the opinion section of *The New York Times*: "Busyness serves as a kind of existential reassurance, a hedge against emptiness; obviously your life cannot possibly be silly or trivial or meaningless if you are so busy, completely booked, in demand every hour of the day. . . . I can't help but wonder whether all this histrionic exhaustion isn't a way of covering up the fact that most of what we do doesn't matter."[69]

I think Tim is dead-on.

Our lives are moving at a frantic pace. In fact, most of us are busy *being busy*: soccer practice twice a week, that big meeting on Monday, choir practice on Wednesday, date night on Friday . . . grocery shopping, bills to pay, vacations to plan, meals to make, emails to send . . . *busy, busy, busy*. Here's another sad reality: Even our kid's lives are scheduled down to the half hour. School activities, clubs, sporting events, day care, play dates. (They return home at night as tired as us!)

And along the way, we're becoming more and more disconnected—from our families, from our friends, from our coworkers, even from ourselves.

We commute to work on freeways, or we telecommute through the internet. We spend countless hours plugged in, staring at computer screens—surfing, emailing, texting, tweeting . . . but not really interacting. We live in single-family homes or condos where we rarely talk to our neighbors, let alone know their names.

Just look around: The world is way different from how it was when we were kids. And just imagine how it was for our grandparents and great-grandparents. A hundred years ago, most people lived on farms or in rural communities where people felt more connected to one another. They shared consistent, socially-agreed-upon values and standards.

Today, the lines aren't all that clear . . . life isn't so black and white.

✓ **Stress-Buster Trick #2:** Self-awareness is very important in over-coming stress. You need to be aware of when you are stressed and understand how your body responds to stress. This will help make it easier to identify the best solution to help you overcome stress.

✓ **Stress-Buster Trick #3:** Our brains are built to deal with stress that only lasts less than a minute. If you find yourself becoming stressed, the best thing to do is to calm yourself down in order to be more focused. Staying focused will help make it easier to overcome any challenges that might come your way.

We are flooded with messages exhorting us to be perfect—or that we will be perfect if we buy the "right" item—reinforcing val-ues of consumerism, materialism, and instant gratification that only serve to amplify the void many of us feel in our lives.[70]

Here's what bothers me the most: *We're out of tune and anxious.*

Anxiety expert Edmund Bourne, Ph.D., explains it this way: "Faced with a barrage of inconsistent world views and standards presented by the media, we are left with the responsibility of hav-ing to create our own meaning and moral order. When we are unable to find that meaning, many of us are prone to fill the gap that's left with various forms of escapism and addiction. We tend to live out of tune with ourselves and thus find ourselves anx-ious."[71]

Using Natural Remedies to Help Relieve Stress

Frankly, I believe there's too cavalier of an attitude toward anxiety meds. We often hear people say, "Oh, yeah, I'm on my Prozac, my Valium, my Xanax," . . . just pick the pill of choice and fill in the

A MINDFUL APPROACE TO RELIEVING STRESS

Engage Your Five Senses to Defeat the Stress Monster

SMELL	▶ The sense of SMELL can have a powerful influence on our moods. ▶ Studies show that after simply inhaling the aroma of jasmine tea for five minutes, participants had slower heart rates and calmer moods.	▶ The smell of flowers, perfume, and the ocean have had amazing impacts on me. ▶ The smell of freshly baked bread, or my favorite, the smell of chocolate chip cookies fresh out of the oven.
SIGHT	▶ The sense of SIGHT can also have calming effects on stress. ▶ Simply seeing a clear, totally blue sky can have a calming effect. ▶ Seeing plants at home or in the office may promote more relaxation.	▶ Looking at photo albums, especially shots of loved ones or images from vacations, can calm the nerves as well as a steaming cup of chamomile tea! ▶ Gazing at a seascape or a greenspace can bring about instant calm.
TASTE	▶ The sense of TASTE is perhaps one of the best stress reducers. ▶ For me it is eating those freshly baked chocolate chip cookies!	▶ Research has found that eating dark chocolate enhances certain chemicals in the brain that can dull pain and give you boost in mood! ▶ Eating something that I really enjoy always changes my mood. ▶ Certain foods can enhance serotonin levels, which can help boost self-esteem.
SOUND	▶ The sense of SOUND can relax you with your favorite music!!! ▶ Sitting in the dentist chair with soothing music in the background relaxes me.	▶ Listening to my favorite music when working out always makes me more positive!
TOUCH	▶ Sense of TOUCH! ▶ Sometimes a simple touch from a loved one can instantly change your mood. ▶ A big hug really works wonders!	▶ Studies show that the act of hugging increases oxytocin levels and diminishes stress levels.

blank. Sometimes we treat an anxiety drug like a status symbol. But if we care about our bodies (flip back to our discussion in Chapter 7), we need to be careful about what we are putting into them. The best solution: Pursue a natural route first. Sometimes, taking pharmaceutical drugs for anxiety treatment is simply unavoidable. But we'd be wise to make this our last resort. Why?

In addition to being addictive, over time—and depending upon the dosage—some anxiety meds can cause increased anxiety, depression, digestive disturbances, sleep problems, loss of sex drive, nervousness and other effects that should not be a result of a health aid. (Don't miss "Avoiding Brain Poisons," an eye-opening story I share at the end of this chapter.)

Herbs are plant-based medicines that are safer, healthier options. Did you know that more than 25 percent of current prescription drugs are based on herbs? Here are three of my favorites:

Some extreme cases of anxiety are nonresponsive to either synthetic or natural remedies. But for many people who suffer from mild to moderate anxiety, these natural remedies can make a real difference. Before you choose drugs that may impart an effect you don't want, give these a try. But if you head to your family physician and explain your symptoms . . . and if he or she instantly pulls out a prescription pad and begins jotting down a pharmaceutical drug solution, you need to speak up. Ask this: "Do you have any other intervention ideas that are organic and natural; solutions that I can try at home?"

If there's simply no way around taking an anxiety drug, talk to your doctor about using medications as a temporary solution. Try it until you can incorporate other stress-relieving strategies. Perhaps it's because of past trauma or physiological issues, but for some people medication is the only effective solution. If this describes your situation, don't feel guilt and shame because you're taking medi-

Herb	Medical Uses	Precautions
Kava *Available Forms:* concentrated liquid extract, capsules, tablets	• A natural tranquilizer • Treats mild to moderate anxiety • Performs as well as the benzodiazepine class of drugs (Valium, Xanax) • Small doses produce a sense of well-being • Large doses produce drowsiness and reduce muscle tension • It is not addictive	• If you have liver problems, do not take kava • Avoid combining with tranquilizers such as Xanax or Klonopin • Avoid alcohol while taking kava
Passionflower *Available Forms:* liquid extract, capsules, tablets	• A natural tranquilizer • Used for nerve-calming purposes • As effective as valerian • Relieves nervous tension and relaxes muscles • Higher doses can be used to treat insomnia	• Just because this is a natural herb does not mean that it is risk-free • Consult your physician before using this herb
Lemon Balm *Available Forms:* liquid extract, capsules, tablets	• Improves mood and boosts both calmness and alertness • Enhances sleep when used with other herbs such as valerian, hops, and chamomile • When used as a calming, relaxing tea, it imparts a tranquil feeling in minutes	• Use with caution • Seek the advice of your physician, and tell him or her about other medications you are taking

cation. Follow your physician's advice and incorporate the strategies I've highlighted in this chapter.

EMPLOYING STRETCHING, DEEP BREATHING, AND MEMITATION TECHNIQUES

As you can see, stress begins in our minds and then works its way throughout the entire body, making us feel tight and tense. Our blood flow is restricted, which creates tension in our lower backs, as well as in many of the other muscles in our bodies. That's why, when anxiety hits, our minds aren't just cloudy; our whole bodies feel out of balance.

Thankfully, getting back in tune isn't that hard. My plan involves a combination of revitalizing stretches, essential breathing, and calming memitation techniques. Following the steps I've presented here can help stimulate your nervous system and decrease the production of those dreaded stress hormones that are bringing you down. The result: a clearer mind and total body relief.

Memitation Definition

I came up with my own stress-reducing technique that combines a mental workout with meditation. I call it "memitation." Officially, it's the act of reviewing memorized information in quiet thought, while focusing on breathing.

I've discovered that the combination of deep, rhythmic breathing while engaging in a memory activity clears my mind

> and enables me to achieve an emotionally calm state. The key: Breathe slowly and deeply. I usually concentrate on the air flowing in and out, deep from my gut, for about three minutes. Then I focus on a positive thought or a positive experience in my life. Soon into my exercise, I begin to review something that I previously committed to memory. This not only relaxes me, but it also reduces stress and anxiety.

Memitation Overview

Three Simple Moves for a Better Mind

1. *Stretch.* From a stiff neck and a tension headache to knotted shoulders and an aching lower back, certain muscles hold stress. So begin by spending three minutes isolating tension-storing muscles—specifically your shoulders, lower back, and neck. Try to hold each stretch for at least 10 seconds and preferably 30 seconds or longer. The pain-relieving benefits will increase the longer you hold these stretches. Rather than rush through the moves. Instead, use this stretching time as a chance to relax and renew. Don't forget to breathe!

2. *Breathe.* Next, as you spend time stretching, tie in deep breathing with each maneuver. Proper breathing is essential to good health and a key to releasing stress and negativity. Medical doctors agree that most of us don't breathe properly. The culprit, of course, is stress. As we explored earlier in this chapter, we feel anxious, worried, frightened, or any number of other emotions that may cause us to hold our breath or breathe irregularly. "Breathing is affected by our emotional state," explains Mark Liponis, M.D., "and our breathing

in turn affects our emotional state. It's quite common, for example, for doctors to find patients complaining of heart attack symptoms in the emergency room only to discover they are simply not breathing properly."[72] In this phase of the exercise, and as you move into the next, make sure you're sitting comfortably in a quiet, calming environment—away from screaming kids, blaring TVs, and buzzing cell phones. If your space checks the box as a stress-free zone, it's time to begin.

3. *Memitate.* Finally, move on to one these memitation techniques: (1) Recall memorized facts. (2) Walk your mind through a relaxing experience. (3) Meditate on meaningful writings that you've committed to memory.

Memitation Daily Plan

Your At-Home or At-the-Gym Daily Routine

Step 1: Stretch

Stretch Your Shoulders

Posture Paradise. This move helps increase circulation and blood flow, moving the spinal column and soft tissues to an upright postural position. The result: reduced stress.

▶ Begin in a standing position, lowering your head and moving it slightly forward in a slouching position.

▶ Next, overcorrect to an upright position with a slight bend to the upper back (without putting pressure on the neck or lower back). Place your thumb between your shoulder blades to make sure you're feeling the movement in the right place: your upper back and shoulder blades.

► Repeat 3 to 5 times in each direction.

Behind-the-Back Resistance Move. The back-and-forth movement of this dynamic shoulder stretch not only engages the rotator cuff, but it also helps ease tension in tight chest muscles.

► Grab a resistance band or roll up a towel lengthwise and grip an end in each hand.
► Hold the band or towel in front of you at waist height and pull your hands apart to create tension.
► Keeping your arms straight, raise the band or towel overhead and lower it behind you. The wider your hands, the easier that will be.
► Reverse the movement to return to the starting position, and repeat.
► Do this up to 10 times.

Stretch Your Neck

Seated Neck Relief. Use your hands to offer a deep stretch for the back of your neck and your upper back.

► Sit comfortably in a chair or on the floor. Clasp your hands and bring both palms to the back of your head. Sitting with a tall spine, ground your hips firmly into your seat.
► From here, begin to gently press your hands down toward your thighs, tucking your chin into your chest. As you press down, use the heels of your palms to pull your head away from your shoulders. This will intensify the stretch even more.

▶ Hold here for at least 30 seconds, and then slowly lift your head up and release your hands.

Behind the Back Standing Stretch. You can do this stretch anywhere, so it's a good one to add to your on-the-go arsenal. It will offer a deep stretch in the sides of your neck.

▶ Stand with your feet hip distance apart, arms by your sides. Reach both hands behind your backside, and hold on to your left wrist with your right hand.

▶ Use your right hand to gently straighten your left arm and pull it away from you slightly. To increase the stretch in your neck, slowly lower your right ear toward your shoulder.

▶ Stay here for 30 seconds and then switch sides.

Stretch Your Lower Back

Child's Pose. This common yoga posture gently stretches the muscles of the lower back, which are likely contracted if you're in pain.

▶ Begin on your hands and knees on the floor, with your hands under your shoulders and knees under your hips.

▶ Reach out directly in front of you, extending your arms and placing your palms flat on the floor.

▶ Slowly sit your hips back toward your heels, dropping your head and chest downward as your arms extend further. If this stretch is too much, place a pillow under your belly to prop yourself up a bit and lessen the stretch of the low back muscles.

▶ Stay here 20 to 30 seconds or even longer.

Knee-to-Chest Stretch. Similar to the other stretches here, this move lengthens contracted lower back muscles.

▶ Begin by lying on your back with your knees bent and feet flat on the floor. Bring your hands to rest either behind your knees or right below your kneecaps.

▶ Slowly bring both knees toward your chest, using your hands to gently pull your knees.

▶ Hold here 20 to 30 seconds, then return to starting position.

Step 2: Breathe

▶ Close your eyes and start breathing naturally. Don't worry about controlling your pace or intensity or any other detail of how you draw air into and out of your lungs; simply breathe normally.

▶ After a few seconds of natural breathing, inhale deeply, hold it, and then slowly let it out. As you do this, focus your thoughts on how your body moves with each breath. Pay attention to your chest, shoulders, rib cage, and tummy.

▶ Take another deep breath. This time, imagine that the air flowing into your lungs is filling you with calm, peaceful feelings. Imagine that the air flowing out is releasing stress and negativity.

▶ As you inhale, say in your mind, "I'm breathing in peace." As you exhale, tell yourself, "I'm letting go of stress."

▶ Pay attention to the four stages of breathing: inhalation, plateau, exhalation, plateau.[73] Try to prolong exhalation and savor the peaceful relaxation of the expiratory plateau.

▶ Continue this deep breathing exercise for five minutes or so, and then move into the final phase.

Step 3: Memitate

Exercise Option 1: Recall Memorized Facts

▶ With your eyes still closed, and continuing to breathe deeply, recall facts, figures, or other information you've committed to memory. For example, I memorized all fifty U.S. states in alphabetical order. So I began recalling the name of each state, starting from the beginning of the alphabet: *Alabama, Alaska, Arizona, Arkansas, California, Colorado, Connecticut, Delaware* . . .

▶ A variation on this exercise is to tie images into each bit of information you recall. Using my example above, I visualized a map of the United States. But instead of recalling the names of each state in alphabetical order, I began at one end of the country (the Pacific Northwest) and picked them off one by one: *Washington, Oregon, California, Montana, Idaho, Nevada* . . . I pictured the shape of each state as I named them.

▶ If necessary, repeat this exercise or, in the same fashion, recall other facts you've memorized.

Why It's an Effective Brain-Booster:
✓ Clears the mind
✓ Promotes an emotionally calm state
✓ Relieves stress
✓ Challenges the brain

Exercise Option 2: Walk Your Mind through a Relaxing Experience

► With your eyes still closed, and continuing to breathe deeply, recall a special memory—an event, a vacation, an experience with someone you're close to. Remember meeting a fiftysomething businessman in Chapter 5—a technology VP named Tyler? His favorite Memitation exercise involves recalling a memory he shared with his wife. The couple celebrated Tyler's fortieth birthday exploring a secret cove on a Caribbean beach. Let's follow Tyler through his memory.

► As Tyler slowly inhaled and exhaled, he allowed his mind to walk through every detail of that memory—the sights, sounds, smells, and emotions.

Why It's an Effective Brain-Booster:

✓ Promotes an emotionally calm state

✓ Relieves stress

✓ Sharpens memory

Exercise Option 3: Meditate on Encouraging Words and Meaningful Writings that You've Committed to Memory

► With your eyes still closed, and continuing to breathe deeply, recall content that you've committed to memory. What kind of content? Anything that is meaningful to you: poems, compelling quotes, a passage of scripture from the Bible, or other religious writings,

► For example, you could recall, repeat, and ponder this encouraging reminder from diarist Anne Frank: "Everyone has inside them a piece of good news. The good news is you don't know how great you can be! How much you can love! What you can accomplish! And what your potential is."

Why It's an Effective Brain-Booster:

✓ Clears the mind

✓ Promotes an emotionally calm state

✓ Relieves stress

✓ Challenges the brain

MEMITATION ON-THE-GO

Ideal at the Office or in the Air

This technique is perfect for limited moments at the office, during a commute, in the air, or at the hotel while you're on the road.

Let's review what memitation is all about and how to do it.

▶ I came up with my own stress-reducing formula by combining a mental workout with meditation. I call it memitation: This is the act of reviewing memorized information in quiet thought, while focusing on breathing.

▶ Breathing slowly and deeply is so important. I usually concentrate on the air flowing in and out, from deep in my gut, for about three minutes, and then I focus on a positive experience in my life and begin to review something that I previously put to memory. This not only relaxes me, but also reduces stress, by lowering cortisol levels. (I once got out of a stressed-out mood by just reviewing the 50 states.)

▶ Memitation also triggers the release of adenosine, the neurotransmitter that makes you tired and promotes sleep. In fact, I practice my zip codes before going to sleep. (This is way better than counting sheep!)

THINKING CREATIVELY, UNLOCKING INTUITION

As I explained in Chapter 5, creative thinking and intuitive inspiration has helped successful people in all walks of life to dream, innovate, and make their mark on the world. You can too. You came into the world with the same potential as some of history's greatest minds: Leonardo Da Vinci, Nicolaus Copernicus, Albert Einstein, Marie Curie, Jane Goodall, Jane Austen, Georgia O'Keeffe—the list goes on and on. Inventors and artists such as these developed techniques to call upon their genius minds to create completely new ideas and turn them into reality. Let's explore a few of their secrets.

According to Edward de Bono, Ph.D., one of the world's leading authorities in cognitive studies, we have two choices when it comes to thinking:

1. Thinking is a matter of intelligence. Intelligence is determined by the genes with which you were born.
2. Thinking is a skill that can be improved by training, by practice and through learning how to do it better. Thinking is no different from any other skill and we can get better at the skill of thinking if we have the will to do so.[74]

After reading my story, I hope you're inspired to dream big, to pursue change . . . and to never limit your thinking. Even if we don't feel smart enough, or strong enough, or young enough, we can change. We can improve. And regardless of our IQ, as Dr. de Bono points out, we can improve our lives by improving our thinking skill.

Just look at my life for proof. I had MIT- or Harvard-level potential, yet I was fooled by the labels people slapped on me. I believed all the lies I was told and made every effort to live up to the reputation of being a loser. I was shy and backward, and after high school, my circumstances didn't change much. I got a job in Allentown, Pennsylvania, as a steelworker . . . only to face forty-year-old bullies on the factory floor. (Go back and reread Chapter 3.)

While there didn't seem to be anything remarkable about my life, I had hope . . . and a head full of dreams and a heart filled with passion. Deep inside, I knew my life could be better. And as you recall from my story, I learned that improving my brain was the first step toward improving my life. Let me repeat one more time a message that echoes throughout these pages: *Change is possible for every man and woman—regardless of our age and our circumstances.*

Today, I'm learning how to unlock greater intuition and creativity.

Today, I'm learning how to . . .

Think Like Leonardo da Vinci, William Shakespeare, and Albert Einstein

Leonardo: Be More Curious. According to historians, there are two questions that Leonardo often asked himself: "What if?" and "How come?"

Asking "what if" requires our brains to project into the future, and it helps us see opportunities where we may have otherwise missed them; it helps us make connections, and it is a way to get our brains more goal-oriented. *What if I started a conversation with this person? What if I tried this new activity? What if I started that new workout program?*[75]

The other question—"how come"—moves us into "why." Instead of passively observing the world or going into automatic responses, we begin to question both our actions and other's motives.

This line of questions forces us to live more purposefully—just as Leonardo did. He refused to waste a second of his life. "How come" helps us to use every second of our life with a mission.[76]

Shakespeare: Be More Creative. While I'm obviously a big advocate of learning through memorization, William Shakespeare has shown us another equally important way of gaining knowledge: learning by heart. In other words, engaging the senses and the emotions as we learn. Shakespeare—like some of history's greatest creative minds—possessed three other qualities that set him apart: He was

1. *An autodidact*—he liked to teach himself, rather than be spoon-fed information or knowledge in standard educational settings.
2. *A polymath*—someone interested in a wide range of subjects. Michelangelo and Leonardo da Vinci were prime examples, as well.
3. *Extremely persistent*—even when confronted with skepticism or rejection.

Nancy C. Andreasen, M.D., Ph.D., is a psychiatrist and neuroscientist who studies creativity extensively. She had the opportunity to scan the brains of thirteen of the most famous scientists, mathematicians, artists, and writers alive today. She also studied the structural and functional characteristics of their brains using neuroimaging. Here's an observation from that study: "Some people see things others cannot, and they are right, and we call them creative geniuses," she explains. "Some people see things others cannot, and they are wrong, and we call them mentally ill. And some people, like John Nash, are both."[77]

Einstein: Be More Visual. In a landmark survey of the working methods of great scientists and mathematicians, Jacques Hadamard,

Ph.D., found that their thinking process was characterized not by language or standard mathematical symbols, but rather by visual imagery. This was clearly the case with Einstein, who participated in the survey. "The words of the language, as they are written or spoken, do not seem to play any role in my mechanisms of thought," he wrote, adding that his own processes instead "rely, more or less, on clear images of a visual and some of a muscular type."[78]

LET'S TAKE OUR MINDS TO THE NEXT LEVEL

With a solid understanding of my Memory Magic plan, we look at ways it can be applied to specific people: students, teachers, business professionals, law enforcement, and military personnel. Most important of all, how can my plan be applied to your life? How will it transform you—your mind, your body, your emotions?

My Memory Magic Plan: At-a-Glance Steps
Brain-Booster No. 5: Increase Creativity and Intuition

- Clear Away Stress and Negativity
- Employ Stretching, Deep Breathing and Memitation Techniques
- Think Creatively, Unlock Intuition

Avoiding Brain Poisons

A Case Against Mind-Numbing Drugs

When we're stressed, we try to cope by escaping. That's what I did (mainly with a poor diet) during my young adulthood. It's these seemingly innocent steps that can get us into trouble.

Anxiety expert Edmund Bourne, Ph.D., explains it this way: "Faced with a barrage of inconsistent world views and standards presented by the media, we are left with the responsibility of having to create our own meaning and moral order. When we are unable to find that meaning, many of us are prone to fill the gap that's left with various forms of escapism and addiction. We tend to live out of tune with ourselves and thus find ourselves anxious."

Ouch! Did Dr. Bourne just describe you? Everything but the addiction part, right? Think again. He goes on to say that we are separated from our own hearts and souls by a variety of addictions, ranging from alcohol and drugs to work, caretaking, or money and material goods.[79]

From Escapism to Addiction

Case in point: Meet forty-two-year-old Matt Samet. So how did he handle an adrenaline-filled lifestyle? With a multitude of diversions, distractions . . . even drugs.

This Coloradan has been rock climbing for more than thirty years and loves it, *craves* it. Yet he insists that climbing is the cause of and the cure for all his maladies.

He says it's the thing that made him obsessive, anorexic, and so anxious that he really thought he needed pills just to cope—most notably, benzodiazepine ("benzo") tranquilizers like Ativan, Klonopin, and Xanax. Through the years, he has abused his body and mind with a variety of other poisons: alcohol, marijuana, muscle relaxants, opiates, mood stabilizers, antipsychotics, coffee, sugar, computer games. Fueled by his hunger for climbing—and his fear of it—he wanted to drink it all in.

"Along the way, I've seen the insides of four psychiatric hospitals, starting in 1986, at age 15," he told *Outside* magazine. "I destroyed my car's steering column and stereo, a countertop, a cell phone, a pinkie finger, and two computers in fits of chemical rage. I've also touched heaven. I've scampered across long alpine ridges solo, gone high up and 'ropeless' on overhangs."

As Matt explained it, "climbing and addiction are ultimately the same disease." And the two nearly claimed his life.

Here's Matt's story in his own words:

A Rock Climber's Toughest Challenge[80]

I first climbed at age twelve, in the Cascades with a family friend, who didn't mind schlepping an overzealous city kid up the gentle but broken peaks. When I was 15, back home in Albuquerque, New Mexico, my parents—divorced five years but not estranged—transferred me from a cushy private school to our district's central-city public school. (I was a fledgling skater who kept getting into trouble.) As I walked those clamorous halls, with my guard always up, a clutching paranoia set in: With my little mohawk, safety-pin earrings, and bourgeoisie "street smarts," I was no match for the real toughs, gangs of whom had already jumped us skater kids on the streets. I stopped attending class—my anxiety too strong to overcome—and my parents rebelled at my rebellion. Two weeks inside a mental hospital (and five months as an outpatient) converted my fear into a manageable panic, but I still saw the world as a place of violent, elemental chaos. I began to climb regularly then. I loved it. On the rocks, the rules were clear and fair, the goals immediate.

Even so, the anxiety never left, and for many years I fed it by depriving my body of food. In my twenties, I wanted to stay skinny for rock climbing because I'd become good enough to aim higher, quickly doing 5.13 and 5.13⁺ routes. In 1991, I moved to Boulder, the nexus of all things body-obsessed and vertical, and kept to a Spartan diet: nonfat hot cocoa, three apples, and 20 saltines per day. I dropped to 125 pounds—this on what was once a stocky five-seven, 165-pound Russian frame. After a year, my heart began to skip beats. With the palpitations came panic attacks, the first one landing me in the ER at age 21, in 1992.

The fear hit then: unprovoked fits of hyperventilating, heart-slamming terror arriving randomly. That's when I discovered benzos, taking a few prescribed Ativan every month. For most people, they're okay for only a couple of weeks. But if you take them daily for a longer period—especially the high-potency variety like Klonopin—you can easily start a cycle of tolerance, addiction, dosage increases . . . and anxiety.

By July 2004, I was taking three milligrams of Klonopin per day, the equivalent of 60 milligrams of Valium. Two pitches up the airy Don Juan Wall, at the Needles, with California's sequoia-studded Kern River Valley spinning 5,000 feet below, I decided I wasn't up to leading, and that it was time to descend. Michael, a close friend and talented free soloist, offered to take over, but I was done. I lowered to his ledge and gobbled a blue-green Klonopin.

"What's up with that?" he asked, pointing at my hand. I took out the bottle and showed him. I told Michael of my anxiety burden, that my doctor said I'd need the pills for the duration. He winced, pinned on the wall with a pill popper.

Later he told me, as he watched me struggle to kick the

habit, "I had to wonder, with you being a climber. It's like, 'Now, how does this work?'"

◆

Matt began asking himself that same question over and over. The very thing he was trying to escape—anxiety—was growing worse.

"Once I quit benzos, I looked at my life," he says. "I looked at things I didn't want or need and were causing me anxiety. Why should I do this anymore? I recently left my job because I was working 60–90 hours a week. That would cause anyone anxiety. I decided I wasn't going to commute. I don't like to fly. Instead of getting on the plane, taking a pill, and practicing my breathing, I'm just not going to fly. I don't need it. It doesn't need me. I'm sick of traffic jams. I'll stay out of the cities. Exercise is a huge help. Even long walks with my dog are good. It sounds like a cliché, but walking with my dog for a few hours a day has been some of the best therapy I've found."

There Is a Better Way

After hearing Matt's story, I was ready to throw out every pill in my own medicine cabinet, even aspirin! He makes a solid anti-drug case: Pharmaceutical medications should be used with the utmost care. *Abuse them, and you're playing Russian roulette with your life.*

As a memory expert—and someone who has seen lives torn apart by the misuse of drugs, prescription and otherwise—I advise extreme caution. Whether or not we're willing to admit it, we have a lot in common with Matt. The same psychological, neurological, and spiritual dynamics of full-fledged addiction are actively at work in every human being. Gerald G. May, M.D., says this: "The same processes that are responsible for addiction to alcohol and narcotics are also responsible for addiction to ideas, work, relationships, power, moods, fantasies, and an endless variety of other things. We are all addicts in every sense of the word."[81]

So viewing medication as a cure-all for worry and stress is a mistake.

I believe we must do much more than relieve the symptoms of what's bugging us; we must get to the cause. We have to address the problem at its source, especially what's driving our adrenaline-filled lives. Also, we must evaluate five key aspects of our lives:

Our Diet: Are we getting the nutrition we need?

Our Aerobic Health: Are we getting regular aerobic exercise?

Our Need for Relaxation: Are we making ample time for rest and relaxation?

Our Need for Sleep: Are we getting the sleep we need every day?

Our Overall Lifestyle: Are we pursuing a less driven, more balanced life?

Now for the flipside of this issue: While anxiety meds aren't the cure-all, they're often a *must* for those who struggle with severe cases of anxiety—especially at the beginning of a wellness program. (So I'm not throwing out my aspirin—and neither should you!) Those battling panic disorder, agoraphobia, obsessive-compulsive disorder, and post-traumatic stress disorder can benefit tremendously from the right pharmaceutical drug.

My advice? Talk with your family physician and a licensed therapist. Get a complete physical and full evaluation. And to help you take that step, my intention here is not to present a debate with one side attempting to prove the other side wrong. On the contrary, I want you to be aware of multiple solutions for improving your mind . . . and changing your life.

Nine Ways to Eliminate Stress and Improve Our Thinking

+ *Identify* the source of stress and negativity.
+ *Discern* fearful thoughts that are excessive or distorted and that have very little basis in reality.
+ *Change* what's within your control.
+ *Let go* of what's out of your control, and learn to be okay with this.
+ *Catch* negative thoughts and replace them with positive ones.
+ *Accept* yourself as you are, knowing that it's perfectly acceptable to perform at your own level instead of someone else's.
+ *Face* tasks that push you out of your comfort zone, but release those that are distractions or that just aren't necessary.
+ *De-shame* the fear of failing, of being blamed for something, of making a mistake, of having a life-controlling struggle, etc.
+ *De-clutter* by reducing busy schedules and striving to simplify life.

Afterword

First Steps Toward a Better New You

Thoughts are very powerful. They can make your mind and your body feel good, or they can make you feel bad. Every cell in your body is affected by every thought you have.[82]

—Daniel G. Amen, M.D.

Congratulations for sticking with my program and completing *Ultimate Memory Magic*! Even though these are the last few pages of my book, in all honesty, you are just getting started. You have taken the first crucial steps toward a fresh start . . . and a better new you. And I'm confident that in the weeks and months ahead you will begin to experience dramatic change:

- Clearer thinking and a sharper mental edge
- The chance to live free from disease
- The best physical shape of your life
- A way to escape negativity and stress
- Much more creativity

As I've shown you throughout this book, a war is being waged inside our bodies—from aging immune systems and increased stress to decreased memories. A myriad of weapons are attacking us on so many fronts. Yet you've discovered with me that there *is* hope.

We really can reverse the damage.

My own story proves that it's never too late and we're never too old to improve our health. Serious heart conditions, debilitating diseases, sky-high blood pressure, out-of-control cholesterol, obesity—regardless of the issue, we can take that first step and do something positive to reclaim our bodies. It's the same with our minds.

We *can* preserve and even enhance our memory and other aspects of mental function. Concentration, alertness, and the ability to focus can be strengthened, leading to improvements in problem-solving ability, productivity, and even IQ.

Before we wrap up our conversation, it's important to recap some transformational messages we need to take to heart.

✓ **Your Brain Can Improve (I'm Living Proof)**

We began our conversation with three secrets that changed my life: (1) my brain can improve, (2) my health can improve, and (3) my quality of life can improve.

→ **Here's what we learned:** We can reach our goals and remove the barriers that hold us back—things like fear, insecurity, wounds from the past, and especially negativity.

✓ **Myth-Buster: "I'm Not Smart Enough"**

I shared my own journey from unmotivated steelworker to memory expert. I told how I struggled with bullies all through high school. Improving my brain was the first step toward improving my life. And guess what else I learned? Change is possible for every man and woman—regardless of our age and our circumstances.

→ **Here's what we learned:** We can achieve our dreams and become the person we were meant to be. The first step toward growth begins when we change our thinking.

✓ Myth-Buster: "I'm Too Weak"

Twenty years ago, I was a depressed steelworker in Allentown, Pennsylvania—broke, stuck, stressed, and in the worst shape of my life. I learned that as I clear away stress and negativity, and as I get my muscles moving and my heart pumping through exercise, I feel better. And after a vigorous workout, my mind is recharged too.

→ **Here's what we learned:** Clearing away negativity, stress, and anxiety are keys to unblocking our minds and improving our lives.

✓ Myth-Buster: "I'm Too Old"

Through my story you learned that I'm now stronger, smarter, and more alive—in my sixties! It's never too late to improve our bodies and our minds. Nothing is stopping any of us from having a better quality of life. The sad fact is, we are our own worst enemies. We limit ourselves and block all the possibilities before us. Two things have given me the motivational fuel I need to improve: I've learned to think both creatively and boundlessly.

→ **Here's what we learned:** Every one of us can become a better version of ourselves. We can take the steps to begin heading in a positive new direction.

✓ Welcome to the World of Cogmental Intelligence

We headed down a path to a more powerful mind and discovered the importance of nurturing the mind-body-emotions connection. My program focuses on treating our *entire* body.

→ **Here's what we learned:** We can learn to read people better and improve our relationships through (1) self-awareness, (2) self-management, (3) social awareness, and (4) relationship management.

✓ Brain-Booster No. 1: Enhance Memory and Sharpen Focus

We explored brain games that exercise our gray matter, and we discovered that at least one of our weekly brain exercises should involve a game or a puzzle—something that challenges our thinking and requires us to solve a problem . . . and even acquire new information.

→ **Here's what we learned:** We can move our minds from autopilot to active and improve our memories by doing two things: (1) Absorbing new information every day, and (2) challenging our minds.

✓ Brain-Booster No. 2: Rev Up Energy and Self-Esteem

I showed you how to tone your body as you boost your brain. A daily memory regimen in tandem with physical exercise can transform our minds, our bodies, and our overall health. The more we exercise our bodies and our minds, the more we're able to think clearly, feel alert and energetic, and have a markedly increased sense of well-being.

→ **Here's what we learned:** We can achieve a sense of well-being and balance (homeostasis) with a holistic mind-body-emotions plan.

✓ Brain-Booster No. 3: Pinpoint Hidden Motives

We mixed deception detection techniques with Emotional Intelligence for a powerful way to read, relate to, and improve our connections with people—both loved ones and strangers alike.

→ **Here's what we learned:** The hidden messages our bodies communicate—nonverbal language can teach us a lot about what others think and feel.

✓ **Brain-Booster No. 4: Build Better Relationships**

We explored how having the ability to identify and manage the emotional state in others, as well as the ability to effectively manage and control our own thoughts, can improve our interpersonal relationships. I combined these abilities with the skills I've learned as a mentalist, not to mention key aspects of deception detection.

→ **Here's what we learned:** Our relationships can improve as we improve trust, communication, and empathy with those we love and interact with.

✓ **Brain-Booster No. 5: Increase Creativity and Intuition**

In order to improve our brains, and ultimately our lives, we must change the way we think. I showed you how to clear away negativity with Memitation techniques. My goal was to show you how to think creatively and boundlessly, and to see the world the way our greatest minds have seen it.

→ **Here's what we learned:** With creativity, a boundless attitude, and the desire to learn, we can think and create like some of history's greatest minds.

✦

As I said at the beginning of the book, the aim of *Ultimate Memory Magic* is to help you discover and apply your own potential for a more powerful mind, and at the same time, to help you improve your health, your relationships, your career, and your overall quality of life.

According to brain expert (and my good friend) Dr. Daniel G. Amen, it all begins with our thoughts. "Every cell in your body," he says, "is affected by every thought you have."

It's time to change our thinking . . . and transform our lives. Let's get going!

Appendix

Techniques That Improve Memory

Memory Palace

One of my favorite techniques is called Memory Palace. Basically, it's a metaphor for any familiar place that we can easily visualize: Examples include the rooms of our house, the town where we live, a garden, a mountain trail, a path along the beach, or a special vacation spot. Here's the point: Make a familiar place a location in your mind where you can store and recall any collection of information.

Here's a quick overview of how it works:

Memory Palace Overview

- Pick a real physical location that's meaningful and memorable to you—for example, various rooms in your home.
- In your mind, create a highly visual walking path through this place.
- Memorize details of the path—such as stepping through the front door of your home, following a tile hallway that leads to your living room, turning left into that room, and then stopping by your cat who is curled up next to a cozy, crackling fireplace.
- Next, take a sequence of items you want to remember and mentally place them in each room you walk through.
- In the very spot where you placed your item, create a story with a mental image that are both so memorable, you'll never forget them.
- Enhance the memory by exaggerating something about the item you want to remember: A gold watch on a nightstand begins to spin and glow and burst with color.
- Finally, as a way of recalling your list in a precise order, always mentally walk the same path through your memory palace and recreate the same story for each room.

The most important first step with this technique is to pick a location that's very real and very familiar to you, a place you can **envision and mentally walk around with ease.** For my example, I chose a cabin in Colorado's Rocky Mountains. The more details I can add and the more vividly I can imagine my cabin in the woods, the more effective my memorization will be.

The next essential step is to create a mental movie. **Forget visualizing static scenes, as if you're flipping through a photo album. Make each room you imagine come to life in 3-D.** Mentally *move* through the rooms, recalling items in a specific order and seeing what's around you. Pay attention to specific features. What's in each room? Imagine colors, textures, smells, and feelings. Are you warm or cold? Happy or sad?

Analyze the room methodically. In addition to setting a specific path, you should define a specific perspective as you tour a room, such as always looking from left to right, for example.[83] What is the next feature that catches your attention? It may be an antique table in the dining room, or a gold-framed picture on the wall. Continue making mental notes of those features as you go. Each one of them will be a "memory slot" that you'll later use to store a single piece of information.[84]

Keys to Creating Your Path

- As you mentally walk down your path, repeat out loud what you see.
- Pull out a notepad and write down each image.
- Always visualize the details from the same point of view.
- Review your path and practice, practice, practice.

Commit your palace to memory, mentally touring it over and over. Once you're satisfied that the route is imprinted on your mind, it's time to fill each room with the items you want to remember. The process is simple: Take a known image—called the memory peg—and combine it with the item you want to memorize. For me, I wanted to memorize specific dates and events that took place in nineteenth-century Colorado. Here are the items I chose:

MY MEMORY LIST EXAMPLE:

Brief History of Colorado (Late 19th Century)

1850—Colorado Gold Rush Begins	1858—Denver Is Established	1861—Colorado Becomes a Territory	1864—Sand Creek Massacre Scars the Land	1870—Silver is Mined
1876—Colorado Becomes the 38th State	1877—University of Colorado Opens Its Doors	1890—Railroads Come to Colorado	1891—Gold is Discovered in Cripple Creek	1893—A Referendum Gives Women the Right to Vote

Here's how I filled each room of my cabin:

My Memory Palace Example:

- FRONT PORCH: I step onto the front porch of my **1850s**, hand-hewn log cabin and **begin** my tour hearing the clang, clang, clang of rusty **gold rush** mining pans. They hang from the ceiling and are blown about by the **Colorado** wind. I stand in front of a weathered wooden door, turn the knob and step inside the cabin.

- LIVING ROOM: **The first thing I see in the living room is a popping, crackling fire in a wide stone fireplace on the left side of the room. I turn and walk toward it. Above the mantel is an 1858** map of **Denver** with the words, "The Mile-High Town **is established.**" Just to the right is another tattered map nailed to the wall. I spot the words, **"1861—Colorado is organized as a territory."** I spin around and head to a door on the other side of the room. It leads to a bathroom. Just in time!

- GUEST BATHROOM: **Inside, an 1864** razor and various shaving lotions, tonics, and concoctions sit next to a wash basin. Watching over them on the wall is the oil painting of a brave Arapaho chief—a remembrance of a tragedy against the Arapaho and

Cheyenne people: The **Sand Creek Massacre.** After paying my respect, washing my hands, and then drying them on a soft, fuzzy towel, I turn around, step out of the bathroom, turn right and head to the back of the cabin.

- KITCHEN: **I step into a kitchen and notice a shelf with a gleaming 1870** silver tea set, which was crafted from **silver mined** nearby. I pour a cup of peppermint tea and head into another room.

- DINING ROOM: **I take a seat at a long, formal dining table and gaze at a set of 1876** plates with the words printed on them: **"Colorado Becomes the 38th State."** I stand up, spin around and climb a spiral staircase that leads to a loft.

- LIBRARY: **The loft is actually a library that's filled with hundreds of old books. I spot one that reads, "1877 University of Colorado opens its doors,"** and another one with the title, **"1890—Railroads come to Colorado."** I walk across the loft and turn toward the left, rear corner of the cabin. I stand directly in front of a door. *Where does it lead?*

- BEDROOM: **I push open the door and see a bedroom. I step in and immediately notice that the room is dominated by a high, bouncy wrought-iron bed.** An **1891** gold watch on a nightstand to the right of the bed begins to spin and glow and burst with color. It was handmade from **gold that was discovered in Cripple Creek.**

- CLOSET: **I spot a closet with a flowing, vintage dress made of silk. I instantly smile, remembering the 1893 referendum giving women the right to vote.**

FOUR TRICKS TO FINDING ANYTHING

At one time or another, everyone—regardless of age or IQ—misplaces something. Our first essential trick is to accept our humanity and cut ourselves some slack. Once we stop beating up ourselves, we can incorporate this plan into our search . . .

(1) *"Decaffeinate" your emotions.* When we're stressed, adrenaline kicks in and the "flight or fight" takes over. The first thing we need to do is calm down. Deep breathing can help.
(2) *Clear away negative thoughts.* Next, move past those panicky "What if," doomsday scenarios. Once your head clears and your heart stops pounding so hard, you can begin your search.
(3) *Recall the moment when you last saw the object.* Once your thoughts are clear and your mind is relaxed, form a mental image of what you were doing or feeling when you last saw the missing item.[85]
(4) *Retrace your steps.* Write down every place you've been since you specifically last remember the item, maybe even the place before you think you lost it.[86]

Are you ready to build your own Memory Palace? It's easy and fun! The key is to be very detailed with your tour, animate each memory, use visual associations, and practice, practice, practice.

Coin a Memory

Grab a handful of coins, and sort them in order of each year. Beginning with the oldest coin, remember something that happened to you during that year. For example, if a coin was minted in 1987, then do your best to remember an event in your life that happened in 1987. Take time to remember the details of your memory, including your emotions, the people you were with, and ponder why you remember this event. Then move on to the next coin until you have associated a memory with each coin.

A-TO-Z LIST OF FACTS, FIGURES, AND POEMS TO MEMORIZE

"A Dream Within a Dream"—Edgar Allan Poe
Bones—206 adult human bones
Capitals of U.S. States—50 key capitals
Dog Breeds—10 groups of 339 breeds

Engine—memorize the basic components
Flowers—151 types in the USA
"Gunga Din"—Rudyard Kipling
Hall of Famers in the MLB—323 to date
Declaration of Independence—4 parts
The Judicial Branch—list USA's courts
Kings Mentioned in the Bible—42 in all
Living Things—learn the classifications
"The Moon"—Robert Lewis Stevenson
Newton's Laws of Motion—3 of them
Order of Planets—learn each name too
Periodic Table of Elements—118 to learn
Quadratic Formula—learn the equation
"The Road Not Taken"—Robert Frost
Sonnet 18—William Shakespeare
Thermodynamics—memorize the laws
Known Universe—stars, planets, galaxies
Vocabulary—learn a new word every day
World Biomes—7 in all
X-Ray Basics—memorize how it works
Lists of Years—3 millennia to learn
Zip Codes—42,000 in the USA

A-TO-Z LIST OF SKILL-BUILDING IDEAS

Art—take a lesson in drawing or watercolor
Business—accounting, finance, human resources, operations, marketing: pick a topic and learn all you can
Cooking—learn what chefs know
Dancing—from ballroom dancing skills to salsa, there's a lot to discover
Electricity—uncover the basics
Faith—learn about the major world religions
Gaming—build an arsenal of brain-boosting games, from card games to online options
Hobbies—take up a new one that involves fine motor skills
Investing—gain insights into basic fundamentals and formulas
Judicial System—Learn about the courts that interpret and apply the law in a country, state, or an international community

(Continued)

Karate—the martial arts are good for your mind, body, and emotions

Language—learn a new one

Music—play a new instrument or if you don't play anything, give it a try

Natural Resources—study the earth's different biomes, as well as topics that range from geology to oceanography

Outer Space—learn astronomy basics

Pharmaceuticals—explore the world of drugs and how they affect the human body

Quasars—find out more about these distant objects, which are 10 billion light-years away

Real Estate—study the principles of buying and selling property

Sports—take up a new one such as golf, bowling, or tennis

Travel—plan trips to distant lands and learn the tricks of the travel industry

Ultraviolet Radiation—discover what it's all about, along with electromagnetic radiation

Vegetable Garden—grow one

World Wide Web—Dive in and learn the ins and outs of this information system that has changed the world

X-Rays—discover how they work

Yoga—find stress relief in these stretching and breathing techniques

Zoology—learn the classifications of the Earth's species

Techniques for Memorizing Lists

Anchor Association

Here's a great exercise: Memorize the following ten words by associating them with the ten anchors.

COW	BRICK	FISH	DICTIONARY	REFRIGERATOR
BANANA	AMAZON ALEXA	CLOCK	FIREMAN	BIRTHDAY CAKE

1. COW

    The anchor for #1 is SUN

    You might want to imagine a cow getting a sun tan, or the

song "Hey diddle diddle the cat and the fiddle, the cow jumped over the SUN!" (Instead of the moon.)

2.   BRICK
     The anchor for #2 is SHOE
     Imagine walking and all of a sudden there's a brick in your SHOE. Or having a pair of shoes that look like bricks.

3.   FISH
     The anchor for #3 is TREE
     You're walking through an orchard picking apples when you come across a Huge TREE with fish hanging from it.

4.   DICTIONARY
     The anchor for #4 is DOOR
     Imagine the DOOR on your neighbor's house being a giant dictionary! When you open it, instead of entering the house, you see nothing but pages of words in front of you.

5.   REFRIGERATOR
     The anchor for #5 is HIVE
     You just returned home from vacation and open up your refrigerator to find a huge BEEHIVE inside of it! Ouch.

6.   BANANA
     The anchor for #6 is STICKS
     You're at a friend's and everyone is toasting marshmallows, when a few of your friends decide they want to try something different. They begin putting bananas on the end of STICKS and toast them. BANANA STICKS!

7. AMAZON ALEXA

   The anchor for #7 is HEAVEN

   Imagine going to HEAVEN and the voice welcoming you to heaven is the voice of Alexa!

8. CLOCK

   The anchor for #8 is PLATE

   You go to a store to buy a new clock for your home. When you get there, every single clock looks like a PLATE!

9. FIREMAN

   The anchor for #9 is SIGN

   You run outside to see a small fire down the street. When you get there you notice the firemen have SIGNS all over their uniforms/raincoats. From the local meat market to the sporting goods store, they look like NASCAR drivers!

10. BIRTHDAY CAKE

    The anchor for #10 is PEN

    You're at a birthday party and when they bring out the cake, instead of candles, there are PENS sticking out all over the cake!

Jim Karol's Celebrity Mental Matrix

As you've learned so far, the most effective memory techniques are the ones that are fun, that capture your interests, and that incorporate vivid (even silly and outrageous) stories and mental images. That's why I enjoy the Peg System and why I have customized my own versions of this technique. Since I'm a movie buff, I developed an anchor system with 100 names of celebrities. Let me demonstrate. For the sake of our discussion, I'll narrow the list to these eight popular people: *Denzel Washington, Brad Pitt, Tom Cruise, George Fore-man, Harrison Ford, Chris Rock, Sylvester Stallone,* and *Tiger Woods.*

Here are four different ways that I have incorporated this list into creative memory techniques:

Ready for another challenge? Take a look at items 11 to 20. In addition to following the steps above, this time incorporate a memory trick.

11. Bevan	12. Delve	13. Aquamarine	14. Floor Clean	15. Aberdeen
16. Loud Ring	17. Seven Dreams	18. Ate Greens	19. Very Lean	20. Twin Tea

✓ **Memory Trick:** Create a colorful rhyming story that's fun and highly visual. Here's one I came up with for our list of 11 to 20 items above: "When I get to 11, I see a man named BEVAN. When I get to 12, I see a farmer dig and DELVE. When I get to 13, I see AQUAMARINE. When I get to 14, I decide to make the FLOOR CLEAN. When I get to 15, I take a trip to ABERDEEN. When I get to 16, I hear a LOUD RING. When I get to 17, my mind is filled with SEVEN DREAMS. When I get to 18, I ATE GREENS. When I get to 19, I notice my tummy is VERY LEAN. When I get to 20, I pour a cup of TWIN TEA."

1. Denzel Washington	2. Brad Pitt	3. Tom Cruise	4. George Foreman
Washington was the first U.S. president; "Wash-ington//One"	*B* is the second letter in the alphabet; there are two *T*'s in Pitt; "Pitt/Two"	There are three letters in Tom; C is the third letter in the alphabet; "Cruise/Three"	FOUR man; "Foreman/Four"
5. Harrison Ford	**6. Chris Rock**	**7. Sylvester Stallone**	**8. Tiger Woods**
		"Stallone/Seven"	Ate a Tiger!
"Ford/Five"	Hit with a rock at six; "Rock/Six"		Tiger Woods using an EIGHT IRON!

Next, I give each celebrity a playing card:

1. Denzel Washington	2. Brad Pitt	3. Tom Cruise	4. George Foreman
Ace of Diamonds	Two of Hearts	Three of Clubs	Four of Clubs
5. Harrison Ford	6. Chris Rock	7. Sylvester Stallone	8. Tiger Woods
Five of Hearts	Six of Diamonds	Seven of Spades	Eight of Clubs

Since I'm having so much fun with this matrix, I decided to give each one a state of the union (in order from one to eight).

1. Denzel Washington	2. Brad Pitt	3. Tom Cruise	4. George Foreman
Delaware	Pennsylvania	New Jersey	Georgia
WASHINGTON crossing the Delaware River	PITTsburg, PA	CRUISE the Jersey shore	GEORGE/Georgia
5. Harrison Ford	6. Chris Rock	7. Sylvester Stallone	8. Tiger Woods
Connecticut	Massachusetts	Maryland	South Carolina
Harrison FORD / Hart FORD	Chris Rock / Plymouth ROCK, MA	Rocky always needed a doctor (MD) / abbreviation for Maryland	SC has some of the best golf courses in the country!

Finally, I associate a country with each celebrity.

1. Denzel Washington	2. Brad Pitt	3. Tom Cruise	4. George Foreman
Greece	Puerto Rico	Bahamas	Georgia
The first known country in the ancient world; WASHINGTON was the first president	PITT/Puerto Rico	CRUISE the Bahamas	GEORGE/Georgia

5. Harrison Ford	6. Chris Rock	7. Sylvester Stallone	8. Tiger Woods
Sudan	Costa Rica	Russia	Greenland
FORD Sudan	CHRIS ROCK / Costa Rica	STALLONE'S *Rocky IV* movie took place in Russia	Tiger putts on the GREEN!

Chunking

This memory technique offers a great method for memorizing long strings of information such as account numbers and passwords. How? By breaking down the information into smaller, more manageable groups or units. For most people, short-term memory can't handle more than seven to nine items at a time. If we try to push beyond nine items, our brains get confused. (Not to sound like a braggart, but I'm one of the few exceptions to that rule!)

Chunking decreases the number of items you are holding in memory by increasing the size of each item. Here's how it works:

+ Let's say this list of numerals is your new bank account number: 3053894625.
+ Instead of memorizing a string of 10 numbers, it will be much easier to remember your account number by grouping or chunking it as "305 389 4625."
+ Essentially, you reduced 10 individual numbers to a manageable group or three larger numbers.

Techniques for Remembering Names, Faces, and Places

Three Ways to Match a Name with a Face

Most of us are pretty good at remembering a face. The struggle comes when we try to match a name with it. Building on the techniques we explored in Chapter 6 (flip back to page 105 for a review), use these three quick tricks to link names and faces and ultimately to lock them into your memory.

1. Link together the face, name, and place in a chain of association.[87]
2. Study a person's face the second you meet them and create a mental caricature, exaggerating various features.
3. Associate the person's name and face to a specific place—work, school, church, etc.

Remember the young teacher named Amy in the opening story of Chapter 6? Before Amy could settle into her new job and begin teaching English to middle schoolers, she needed to quickly learn how to navigate a stressful environment, endure negativity from her boss, break through communication barriers . . . *and* memorize a couple hundred names, plus key details of each person's life.

Here's an example of how she used the three tricks above to match a face with a student named Sofia Valentina Lopez:

First, she studied Sofia's pretty face. As the young girl talked, Amy took note of her bright brown eyes, delicate features, straight black hair, and pink clothes and jewelry she wore.

Second, she created a mental caricature. Amy exaggerated Sofia's eyes and smile.

Finally, she made some key associations: (1) Amy linked Sofia's pretty features, pink outfits, and middle name—Valentina—with a valentine. (2) Amy linked the student with an actress she admired: Sofia Vergara of TV's *Modern Family*. (3) Amy linked the student to a specific school period and row in her classroom.

Whenever Amy sees Sofia in the halls at her school, this chain of association flashes in her mind and she instantly remembers the girl's name.

Two Tricks to Remembering Where You Parked

It's frustrating, and it happens to us all. We step out of a mall (or a sporting event or the airport), make our way into a parking garage, and then we stop dead in our tracks—panic washing over our face. *Where on earth did I park my car?*

Apart from wasting precious time and raising your blood pressure a bit, what can you do to avoid these kinds of annoying scenarios? Try this:

1. The moment you step out of your car, pause and observe your surroundings. Look for landmarks: parking garage elevators, stairwells, a nearby store sign, etc.

2. Before you leave a parking structure and enter the mall (or the airport terminal), pause again and turn around, viewing the parking lot from the other direction. This is what you'll see when you return later. Obviously, if the lot is numbered or named, write it down.

HOW TO STOP MISPLACING YOUR KEYS

It may sound a bit obvious, but here's a big key to *stop* losing your keys: Get in the habit of always putting them in the same place. We lose them when we're stressed, in a hurry, or just plain out of sync with life. So, the best way to stop misplacing them is to establish a routine and stick with it.

1. Find an exact place for your keys and be diligent about putting them there when you don't need them.
2. If you notice them in a different place, take the time to put them in the spot you designated. (Trust me, this will save you from frustration later.)
3. Train family members to honor your designated "key zone" and place them in that spot too.

Math Games to Sharpen Your Thinking

Pattern Recognition

These puzzles are designed to work our executive functions in our frontal lobes by using pattern recognition, hypothesis testing, and logic. The idea is pretty straightforward: Answer this simple question—*What comes next in the sequence?* We'll begin with an easy one, and then we'll turn up the heat with more challenging games. The trick is to solve these puzzles quickly.

PUZZLE # 1: EASY TWO-DIGIT SEQUENCE

10, 15, 25, 30, 40, 45, ___
ANSWER: 10, 15, 25, 30, 40, 45, <u>55</u>
SOLUTION: Add 5, add 10, add 5, add 10, . . .

PUZZLE # 2: MODERATE TWO-DIGIT SEQUENCE

7, 14, 28, 35, 49, 56, ___
ANSWER: 7, 14, 28, 35, 49, 56, <u>70</u>
SOLUTION: Add 7, add 14, add 7, add 14, . . .

PUZZLE # 3: CHALLENGING THREE-DIGIT SEQUENCE

177, 254, 365, 442, 553, 630, ___
ANSWER: 177, 254, 365, 442, 553, 630, <u>741</u>
SOLUTION: Add 77, add 111, add 77, add 111, add 77, add 111, . . .

Mental Math

Doing mental math stimulates our mind and keeps our brains quick and sharp, enabling it to work much more efficiently. As we become more proficient, we'll gain a greater appreciation for how numbers interact, which is helpful when we face complicated math problems. At that point, finding a solution will be far less intimidating!

These exercises will help you improve your mental math skills.

MENTAL MATH #1: HEAD GAME EXERCISE

Add It Up . . .
- In your head, add 1,020 + 1,020.
- Now add 20 to your answer.
- Now add 20 + 10 + 10 to it.

> **What's The Answer?**
>
> Is it 3,000? If that's what you think, you would be absolutely, positively, 100 percent *wrong!* (But you're not alone, because that's what most people think.) Try it again.
>
> **Here's The Real Answer**
>
> 1,020 + 1,020 + 20 + 20 + 10 + 10 = 2,100

Trachtenberg Speed System of Basic Mathematics

Jakow Trachtenberg, a Russian Jewish engineer, developed this method while he was imprisoned in a Nazi concentration camp. At the time, it was the only way he could escape the horrors he encountered daily, not to mention a means he used to keep his mind sharp. But for the rest of the world, the Trachtenberg Speed System of Basic Mathematics became one of the best ways for individuals to perform arithmetic computations very quickly and easily—especially if they want to do it mentally.

This system scales up from single digit multiplication, enabling its users to multiply massive numbers with no change in the method. The basic multiplication method taught in this system is ideal for children and for adults who feel they are poor at multiplying. The rules are easy to learn, and it does not take much practice to become proficient. Here are some basics. (But for a more thorough discussion, visit this website: www.trachtenbergspeedmath.com.)

MENTAL MATH #2: TRACHTENBERG'S EASY METHOD OF BASIC MULTIPLICATION[88]

> The first part of the system involves a set of rules for multiplying any number by the numbers 0 through to 12. It was designed so that users do not need to know the multiplication tables. Solving a problem involves no multiplication at all! Let's explore an example.
>
> **FIND THE ANSWER: 427 × 12 = ____**
>
> Begin by following this rule: *Double the number and add the neighbor.* Here are the steps to follow:

(Continued)

Begin by placing a zero in front of the number you are multiplying, and then underline it.

STEP 1: <u>0427</u> × 12

Beginning on the right, double the 7. It has no neighbor to the right to add.

STEP 2: 7 + 7 = 14 (write 4 and carry 1)

0427 × 12
_____
    4

Moving left to the next column, double the 2 and add the 7, its neighbor, then add the 1 carried over.

STEP 3: 2 + 2+7 + 1=12 (write 2 and carry 1)

0427 × 12
_____
   24

Moving left to the next column, double the 4, and then add its neighbor, 2, and add the 1 carried over.

STEP 4: 4 + 4+ 2 + 1 = 11 (write 1 and carry 1)

0427 × 12
_____
  124

Moving to the last column, doubling zero is still zero, so we ignore this and then add its neighbor, 4, and then add the 1 carried over.

STEP 5: 4 + 1 = 5 (write 5)

0427 × 12
_____
 5124

ANSWER: 5124

The goal is doing mental math without going mental! So, practice doing the computations in your head. Here's an alternative: Write out each digit of the answer as you work it out.

Acknowledgments

I want to express my heartfelt gratitude and indebtedness to my friends and colleagues who helped me shape an idea into an exciting reality:

My mentor, Daniel G. Amen, M.D.—a double-board-certified psychiatrist, teacher, and nine-time *New York Times* bestselling author. Credentials and accomplishments aside, however, it's our longtime friendship and shared vision that means so much to me. Dr. Amen and I are passionate about helping individuals improve their minds and ultimately their lives. Together, we developed a television series and online course called "Jim Karol's Memory Master Course." Dr. Amen's wisdom has had a great impact on this book.

My friends and fellow speakers at the USO tour. I have proudly served as a featured speaker with this amazing organization right alongside my friend, Chef Robert Irvine, host of Food Network's *Restaurant: Impossible*. These events have supercharged my desire to help others.

My manager, Michael Hammond, and my literary agent, Greg Johnson. Michael, your support and direction have taken me places I never dreamed were possible. Greg, you know the "art of the deal." You are the best in the business!

My writer, Michael Ross. His award-winning ability as a journalist and experience creating reader-friendly books has seriously paid off! Thank you, Michael, for pulling stories and concepts out of my head and so skillfully weaving them into these pages.

My wife, Lynn. Without you, none of this matters. I'll never forget first setting eyes on you—my soulmate from Catasauqua, Pennsylvania. You and our kids and grandkids are the bright spots of my life—the greatest blessings of all.

Notes

1. Dr. Archibald D. Hart, *The Anxiety Cure* (Nashville, TN: Thomas Nelson, 2001), 9.
2. Julian Whitaker, M.D., and Carol Colman, *Shed 10 Years in 10 Weeks* (New York: Fireside, 1997), 17.
3. From Mehmet Oz, M.D., Sharecare, 2010–2013, accessed September 18, 2013, www.sharecare.com/health/anxiety/why-anxiety-cause-upset-stomach.
4. Elouise Renich Fraser, *Confessions of a Beginning Theologian* (Downers Grove, IL: InterVarsity Press, 1998), 31.
5. Dr. Archibald D. Hart, *The Anxiety Cure* (Nashville, TN: Thomas Nelson, 1999), 15.
6. For a thorough discussion, read Chapter 2, "The GABA-Anxiety Connection," in Dr. Hart's book *The Anxiety Cure*.
7. Daniel G. Amen, *Change Your Brain, Change Your Life* (New York: Three Rivers Press, 1998), 59–60.
8. Julian Whitaker, M.D., and Carol Colman, *Shed 10 Years in 10 Weeks* (New York: Fireside, 1997), 163.
9. Michael J. Gelb, *Discover Your Genius: How to Think Like History's Ten Most Revolutionary Minds* (New York: HarperCollins, 2002), 2.
10. Ibid.
11. Ibid.
12. Ibid., ix.
13. I highly recommend this website, especially this article: "Effects of Negative Words," Your Dictionary, 2018, http://grammar.yourdictionary.com/style-and-usage/affects-of-negative-words.html.
14. Ken Gu, "How Powerful Is Our Mind," Quora, September 24, 2016, www.quora.com/How-powerful-is-our-mind.
15. Some of these suggestions were adapted from "7 Ways to Jumpstart Healthy Change in Your Life," Harvard Health Publishing, Harvard Medical School, September 2018, www.health.harvard.edu/healthbeat/7-ways-to-jumpstart-healthy-change-in-your-life.

16. Chris Heath, "Your Memories Make You Who You Are," *Psychology Today*, August 8, 2017, www.psychologytoday.com/us/blog/psychoanalysis-unplugged /201708/your-memories-make-you-who-you-are.

17. "Improving Memory," Harvard Health Publishing, Harvard Medical School, accessed September 3, 2018, www.health.harvard.edu/topics/improving -memory.

18. Ibid.

19. Dr. Henry Cloud, *Changes That Heal* (Grand Rapids: Zondervan ,1992), 49.

20. Alexandria Sifferlin, "The Simple Reason Exercise Enhances Your Brain," *Time*, April 26, 2017, http://time.com/4752846/exercise-brain-health/.

21. Ibid.

22. Daniel Goleman, *Emotional Intelligence* (New York: Bantam Books, 1995), 13.

23. Joe Navarro, *What Every Body Is Saying: An Ex-FBI Agent's Guide to Speed-Reading People* (New York: William Morrow, 2008), 1–2.

24. Psalm 19:1–2, Contemporary English Version.

25. Bob Anderson, *Stretching: 30th Anniversary Edition* (Bolinas, Calif.: Shelter Publications Inc, 2010), 9.

26. Kara Leah-Grant, "Why It's Important to Breathe," The Yoga Lunchbox, January 21, 2009, https://theyogalunchbox.co.nz/why-its-important-to -breathe/.

27. Travis Bradberry and Jean Greaves, *Emotional Intelligence 2.0* (San Diego: TalentSmart, 2009), 6.

28. Ibid.

29. David Walton, *Emotional Intelligence: A Practical Guide* (New York: MJF Books, 2012), 21.

30. Whitaker, *Shed 10 Years*, 158.

31. Oscar Ybarra et al., "Mental Exercising Through Simple Socializing: Social Interaction Promotes General Cognitive Functioning," Sage Journals, December 4, 2007, https://doi.org/10.1177/0146167207310454.

32. Ibid.

33. Ceylan Yeginsu, "The U.K. Appoints a Minister for Loneliness," *New York Times*, January 17, 2018.

34. Ibid.

35. Ana Sandoiu, "Do Brain-Training Games Really Work?" Medical News Today, August 1, 2018, www.medicalnewstoday.com/articles/322648.php.

36. See Bobby Stojanoski, *Neuropsychologia*, Volume 117 (August 2018), 541–550.

37. Sandoiu, "Do Brain-Training Games Really Work?"

38. Richard C. Mohs, "How to Improve Your Memory," How Stuff Works: Health, 2018, https://health.howstuffworks.com/human-body/systems /nervous-system/how-to-improve-your-memory8.htm.

39. For a much more thorough discussion on Peg Systems, see "How to Unlock Your Amazing Memory," The Memory Institute, 2018, www.thememoryinstitute .com/the-peg-system.html.

40. "Never Get Lost Again! Tips for Remembering Directions," ImproveMemory .org, 2017, www.improvememory.org/blog-posts/how-to-improve-memory /remember-directions/

41. Whitaker, *Shed 10 Years*, 138.

42. Stephanie Castillo, "The Evolution of the Runner's High: How Endurance Exercises Changes Your Brain," *Medical Daily*, February 27, 2015, www .medicaldaily.com/evolution-runners-high-how-endurance-exercise-changes -your-brain-323734.

43. Ibid.

44. Sara Reistad-Long, "How to Combat Every Kind of Stress," *Women's Day*, February 11, 2013, accessed August 5, 2013, http://healthyliving.msn.com /health-wellness/stress/how-to-combat-every-kind-of-stress.

45. See "Stress: The Silent Killer," Holistic Online, www.holisticonline.com /stress/stress_diet.htm.

46. Don Colbert, M.D., *The New Bible Cure for Sleep Disorders* (Lake Mary, Fla.: Siloam, 2009), 1.

47. Barbara Mantel, "A Good Night's Sleep Scrubs Your Brain Clean, Researchers Find," NBCNews.com, October 17, 2013, www.nbcnews.com/health /good-nights-sleep-scrubs-your-brain-clean-researchers-find-8C11413186 ?ocid=msnhp&pos=3.

48. Barbara N. Vosk, Rex Forehand, and Rolando Figueroa. "Perception of Emotions by Accepted and Rejected Children," *Journal of Behavioral Assessment*, 5, no. 2 (1983): 151–160.

49. Leonard Mlodinow, "How We Communicate Through Body Language," *Psychology Today*, May 29, 2012, www.psychologytoday.com/us/blog/subliminal /201205/how-we-communicate-through-body-language.

50. Paul Ekman, *Emotions Revealed*, 2nd ed. (New York: Times Books, 2003), 14–15.

51. David Matsumoto and Hyi Sung Hwang, "Science Brief: Reading Facial Expressions of Emotion," American Psychological Association, May 2011, www .apa.org/science/about/psa/2011/05/facial-expressions.aspx.

52. For a thorough discussion, see Paul Ekman and Wallace V. Friesen, "Constants across culture in the face and emotion," *Journal of Personality and Social Psychology*, 17, no. 2 (1971), 124–129.

53. David J. Lieberman, Ph.D., *Never Be Lied to Again* (New York: St. Martin's Press, 1998), 20.

54. Emma M. Seppälä, Ph.D., "8 Ways Your Body Speaks Way Louder Than Your Words," *Psychology Today*, April 11, 2017, www.psychologytoday.com/us/blog /feeling-it/201704/8-ways-your-body-speaks-way-louder-your-words.

55. Navarro, *What Every Body Is Saying*, 172.

56. Ibid., 157.

57. David J. Lieberman, *You Can Read Anyone*, (Lakewood, NJ: Viter Press, 2007), 91.

58. Dr. Leo Buscaglia, *Born for Love* (New York: Random House, 1992).

59. Walton, *Emotional Intelligence*, 4–5.

60. Ibid.

61. Bradberry and Greaves, *Emotional Intelligence 2.0*, 141.

62. Bruce Y. Lee, "Here Are the 27 Different Human Emotions, According to a Study," *Forbes*, September 9, 2017, www.forbes.com/sites/brucelee/2017/09/09/here-are-the-27-different-human-emotions-according-to-a-study/#1b9cff761335.

63. Bradberry and Greaves, *Emotional Intelligence 2.0*, 14.

64. Lee, "27 Different Human Emotions."

65. Alex Niles, "What Is Fear," *Psychology Today*, May 19, 2014, www.psychologytoday.com/us/blog/recovery-road/201405/what-is-fear.

66. Martin M. Antony, Ph.D., and Peter J. Norton, Ph.D., *The Anti-Anxiety Workbook* (New York: The Guilford Press, 2009), 26.

67. Ibid.

68. For a thorough discussion, read Chapter 2, "The GABA-Anxiety Connection," in Dr. Hart's book *The Anxiety Cure*.

69. Tim Kreider, "The 'Busy' Trap," *New York Times*, June 30, 2012, http://opinionator.blogs.nytimes.com/2012/06/30/the-busy-trap/?_r=0.

70. Edmund Bourne, Ph.D., *Coping with Anxiety* (Oakland, CA: New Harbinger Publications, Inc., 2003), 8–9.

71. Ibid.

72. Mark Liponis, M.D., *Ultralongevity: The Seven-Step Program for a Younger, Healthier You* (New York: Little, Brown and Company, 2007), 85.

73. Ibid., 95.

74. Edward de Bono, *De Bono's Thinking Course* (New York: Facts on File, Inc., 1994), 1.

75. Michael J. Gelb, *How to Think Like Leonardo da Vinci* (New York: Delacorte Press, 1998).

76. Ibid.

77. Nancy C. Andreasen, "Secrets of the Creative Brain," *The Atlantic*, July/August 2014, www.theatlantic.com/magazine/archive/2014/07/secrets-of-the-creative-brain/372299/.

78. Michael J. Gelb, *Discover Your Genius* (New York: HarperCollins, 2002), 318.

79. Bourne, *Coping with Anxiety*, 8–9.

80. This story was adapted from Matt Samet, "Beauty in the Breakdown," *Outside*, June 7, 2010, www.outsideonline.com/outdoor-adventure/climbing/rock-climbing/Beauty-in-the-Breakdown.html

81. Gerald G. May, M.D., *Addiction and Grace* (San Francisco: HarperCollins, 1988), 3–4.

82. Amen, *Change Your Brain*, 59–60.

83. "Develop Perfect Memory with the Memory Palace Technique," Litemind, https://litemind.com/memory-palace/

84. Ibid.

85. Christopher Mele, "How to Find Your Missing Keys and Stop Losing Other Things," *New York Times*, April 3, 2017, www.nytimes.com/2017/04/03/well /missing-keys.html.

86. "How to Find Something You've Lost (or Misplaced)," Lost Box post, October 21, 2014, https://mylostbox.com/how-to-find-something-youve-lost -or-misplaced/

87. Dominic O'Brien, *You Can Learn to Remember* (London: Watkins, 2014), 116.

88. I encourage you to learn the Trachtenberg Speed System of Basic Mathematics. I adapted this exercise from the Trachtenberg Speed Math website: https://trachtenbergspeedmath.com/.

About The Authors

JIM KAROL

Jim has gone from a steelworker in Allentown, Pennsylvania, to becoming one of the most extraordinary minds in the world! He is like Rocky Balboa meets Rain Man. Jim is a genuine "marvel of the mind" and one of the world's absolutely true mentalists. He has been seen by millions of people from his appearances on the *The Tonight Show*, *Today*, *Howard Stern*, and numerous other television and news programs. In 2007, Jim was featured as one of the world's top ten mentalists, in a weekly live show on NBC called *Phenomenon*. He has also held three Guinness world records, among other accolades. What sets Jim apart from other mentalists in the world is that most of his mental abilities are absolutely real!

Today, Jim's "better mind, better life" message is resonating with people from all walks of life—everyone from Hollywood actors and pro athletes to Ivy League academics and ordinary folks alike. Each year, Jim speaks in a wide range of venues: corporate retreats, medical symposiums, MIT conferences, the Pentagon, the USO Entertainment Tour, Wounded Warrior events, memory competitions, and much more.

Jim lives in Allentown, Pennsylvania.

MICHAEL ROSS

Michael Ross is an award-winning writer and the former editor of *Breakaway*, a national magazine for teenage boys. He is also the author, coauthor, and collaborator of more than forty books for readers of all ages, including an unofficial Minecraft guide for kids, *Block by Block* (Harvest House).

During his writing career, Michael has written and edited thousands of articles and has interviewed hundreds of athletes, musicians, and actors, as well as amazing people from all walks of life. Some of his most memorable interviews include: actors Sylvester Stallone and Stephen Baldwin, director Catherine Hardwicke (*Twilight, Lords of Dogtown*), pop superstar Nick Jonas, rockers Cheap Trick, and contemporary Christian music artists Kirk Franklin, TobyMac, Skillet, and Steven Curtis Chapman.

Michael and his family live in St. Louis, Missouri.